All
in the
Family

All
in the
Family

A SURVIVAL GUIDE FOR
FAMILY LIVING & LOVING
IN A CHANGING WORLD

Betty Jane Wylie

KEY PORTER BOOKS

R006147405O

HQ734 W94
. 1988

Canadian Cataloguing in Publication Data

Wylie, Betty Jane.
  All in the family

ISBN 1-55013-116-8

1. Parenting. 2. Family. I. Title.

HQ734.W94 1988   646.7'8   C88-094342-4

All inquiries regarding the motion picture, television and dramatic rights for this book should be addressed to the author's representative:

The Colbert Agency Inc.
303 Davenport Road
Toronto, Ontario
M5R 1K5

Representations as to the disposition of these rights are strictly prohibited without express written consent and will be vigorously pursued to the full extent of the law.

The publisher gratefully acknowledges the support of the Ontario Arts Council.

Key Porter Books Limited
70 The Esplanade
Toronto, Ontario
Canada M5E 1R2

Design: First Image

Printed and Bound in Canada

88 89 90 91 92 6 5 4 3 2 1

Contents

Acknowledgements

This is not quite the book I planned to write, but I do want to thank the people who helped me with it: Robert Glossop, program co-ordinator of the Vanier Institute of the Family, Jennifer Glossop (his sister-in-law), my favourite editor, and the Burlington Public Library, for assistance and resources.

Dedication

To my surrogate family, Nancie and Art

All
in the
Family

INTRODUCTION

Govern a family as you would cook a small fish — very gently.
— *Chinese proverb*

This book is about you and the people you love. You care so much, but you wonder if you're missing something. It was easier, you think, for your parents. They had accepted patterns and guidelines to follow that don't seem to apply any more. That was then, this is now. You have different problems than your parents had and different expectations.

For one thing, the double income family is here to stay. Bottom lines being what they are, two incomes are an economic necessity for most families today. Mind you, bottom lines are higher than they used to be. Our expectations seem to be on an upwardly sliding scale as yesterday's luxuries become today's necessities. Staying at home with preschool children, for example, has become a luxury and requires a conscious, often agonizing choice.

The divorce rate continues to be high and frightening, as do the prospects on the other side of a settlement: usually straitened circumstances for a female single parent, bitterness for a male denied access to his children. A second marriage brings problems with it, often in the form of children from previous unions. Reconstituted families need new ground rules and stepparents need better press than they've been getting.

1

If you are part of the Sandwich Generation – caught between emotionally and sometimes financially dependent aging parents and children who need you longer than they ever did – the Empty Nest may look like a quiet space you look forward to, but you may feel guilty for feeling that way.

How can you stop feeling guilty? How can you be sure you're doing the right thing? How can you be sure you're having any fun? How can you be sure of anything these days? You just want your children to be safe and happy. You just need more money, more time, and more love.

Money's hard. Financial pressures are squeezing middle-class families into strange shapes and uneasy lifestyles. Solving that problem, two working parents find that time is scarce. Fathers must help and children have to be organized. Fortunately, love is still available.

This book is about the application of love. It is intended to help you come to terms with your expectations as well as with your family, and to suggest sensible, comfortable ways of living and loving in the family in the nineties. Use it well.

PART ONE

What Is a Family?

CHAPTER ONE

Families in History

He that would know what shall be, must consider what hath been.
— *H.G. Bohn, Handbook of Proverbs, 1855*

The family is the basic human institution. Ever since the first human beings holed up in a cave with a fire at its mouth to keep the wild things at bay, they developed certain rules about whose corner of the cave was whose and who got the choicest pieces of meat and how much they were going to feed the old one who was such a drag and whether to hang skins on the walls of the cave or paint pictures on them and what to do about the kid who was taking too many risks in the hunt. In other words, they were working out a lifestyle. That's what you're doing, too.

Don't pay any attention to anyone who tries to tell you that the family is dead or dying. It's just changing – again. Like the farmer's axe that over the years has had three new heads and two new handles, it goes on and on. Stop to consider how it has changed.

The Olden Days

People keep talking about the olden days as if they were golden. Awful things happened to people then (they still do); life was often cheap and usually very short. Only the gods knew where the infants came from, or why, but they kept on coming, and if most of them died, there were more where they came from, wherever that was. Since a female spent most of her adult life either pregnant or lactating, she needed a little help providing for the kids. Thus it was in her own best interests (so say some experts) to be in heat most of the time (unlike animals) in order to attract and service a male to guarantee his protection.

When people settled down to herd or to farm, the herdsmen finally discovered what was causing all those babies. (Take the ram out of the flock and what have ewe?) That's how male chauvinism was born, too. Somehow or other, the males figured they had life-and-death power over the females and the young, so life for a lot of those poor creatures remained cheap and short. Infanticide, particularly female infanticide, was practised for centuries, including during classical Greek and Roman times and up through the Middle Ages, with different methods being favoured. Babies had tough lives and often short ones.

Now the social doomsayers are saying that childhood is dead, that such terrible things are happening to children today that people can't possibly revere children the way they used to, and that families are so fragmented and confused that they are on their way to dead. The way it was was better, they say, ignoring the infant (and maternal) mortality rates of centuries past, turning a blind eye to the child abuse and kiddie porn of "the other" Victorians, a deaf ear to the cries of four-year-old chimney sweeps and nine-year-old miners, and a bland statistic to any odious comparisons that contradict their nostalgia.

What Is a Family?

Ogden Nash said: "A family is a unit composed not only of children, but of men, women, an occasional animal, and the common cold."

Call it a cluster or a pack, a clan or a tribe, a family, as it has developed and changed, is a group of people more or less related by blood who have gathered or been gathered together in a common interest of protection and survival. The Canadian Census defines family as "a married couple with or without never-married children living in the same dwelling, or a lone parent living with one or more never-married children."

(Immediately I want to ask, what about the ones who come back?) Sociologists have their own questions and seek broader definitions.

Here are some definitions (with my comments) from the *Gage Canadian Dictionary*. Where do you fit in?

- A father, mother, and their children

  Right here you get into trouble: are the children the offspring of the original father and mother, who are still married to each other? Or are they members of a reconstituted or blended family: Father Blue, Mother Yellow, with Blue children, Yellow children, and Green children from the new union?

- The children of a father and mother

  Where do these children live? With their single mother, single father, with their stepfather or stepmother, in foster home(s), or, as in some cases I have read of, with each other, bringing themselves up rather than be separated?

- One's spouse and children

  These days one's spouse is not necessarily the parent of all one's children, or even some or one of them. Or maybe the children are the spouse's children and not one's own. Introductions get more difficult all the time.

- A group of related people living in the same house

  People who live in the same house are not always related by blood, as we might mistakenly expect. They can be related by a common interest, as are college students who live together for economy's sake. They can be residents of a group home brought together for communal living while they learn life skills to prepare them to live on their own (ex-convicts, developmentally handicapped, unwed mothers, battered wives and so on). Whatever the reasons that have brought these people together, while they live in the same house they function as a family.

- All a person's relatives

  All the relatives may assemble at special times such as weddings, christenings, bar and bat mitzvahs, funerals, Thanksgiving, Yom Kippur, Hanukkah or Christmas, and sometimes reunions, in order to observe family rituals, additions, departures, celebrations. Some families are closer than others; some celebrate more than others.

- A group of related people, a tribe

Some people are related, for a time at least, by a common cause, ranging from a political interest to a shared concern such as bereavement, divorce, illness, alcoholism, and so on. The idea of tribe was revived by other than native peoples in the sixties, when the flower children banded together in communes (or families). Marshall McLuhan predicted that the media would bring all the peoples of the world back into a tribal situation in a global village. It hasn't happened yet.

- Any group of related or similar things

This definition, of course, refers more to the flora and fauna of the world than to the people who constitute families. In *Slapstick*, Kurt Vonnegut used the idea to create artificial families.

These are all abstract concepts, having very little to do with Real Life as you and I know it in families today. There is no mention in any dictionary of the grim realities families face today as they try to cope day by day by day. What about:

- Double income families? In 1971, 36.9 percent of married women were in the labour force; by 1981, 52 percent of them were out there, and present estimates are passing 65 percent. The fastest growth is among women with children under the age of two. The percentage of childless wives in the labour force has also increased, but not as quickly or as high as that of mothers with dependent children. The reason is strictly financial. A *Toronto Star* survey revealed that if all the married women working outside the home quit tomorrow, the number of families living below the poverty line would double.

- Single parent families? The 1984 Family History Survey showed that of four million families with children under the age of twenty-five, 16 percent were lone-parent families; of these, just over three-quarters of single parents were female. There are three types of lone-parent women: those who have never been in a marriage union; those who are separated or divorced; and those who are widowed. It is estimated that of all the children born in the eighties in North America, one in five will live for a time with only one parent before the age of sixteen.

• Blended families? Not as common as you might think. In view of the bad publicity about the divorce rate, it may come as a surprise to learn that 66 percent of all husbands and wives stay together until death do them part. The blended families come in because 78 percent of all divorced couples remarry, representing, as Samuel Johnson once said, the "triumph of hope over experience."

• Extended families? We talk about the good old days when three generations commonly lived under one roof – one big, happy family. It's about as common today as it ever was: about 6 percent of families comprised three generations in one household, then (in the nineteenth century) as now.

• Co-vivants? Although common-law partnerships have increased in recent years, they are still far from the norm. Only 5.2 percent of males surveyed and 6.5 percent of females reported such an arrangement. (I can never figure out why these numbers don't match.) Common-law partnerships are as frequently a prelude to marriage as a substitute for it.

• Very close friends? These include homosexual couples, both male and female, who live together, as well as people, same or opposite sex, who share accommodation and expenses to ease their finances. If such an arrangement numbers more than two people, then they become:

• Co-ops and communal experiments. Group homes have already been mentioned. I know a number of young, poor theatre people (actors, writers), and other young people just starting out in the big city, who share accommodation until they get a stake. During their time of cohabitation, they behave with each other like "family."

All these patterns of living represent family life in some form today, and each of them presents its own problems. It might help to go back to prototype before we go on to specific problems.

Two Kinds of Family

There are two kinds of family: the family of origin, that is, the one you were born in, and the family of procreation, that is, the one you move into and create with children of your own. Most people have the first, having sprung from somewhere; not everyone, obviously, goes on to the second. (You know that old definition of heredity? Heredity means if your grandfather didn't have children, it's likely your father didn't, and you won't either.) As we know, and will observe, the forms of families may differ a lot.

I invite you to consider carefully your own family of origin. Does it bear any resemblance to a) Upper Canada Village? b) Main Street, U.S.A.? c) mine?

My family of origin was the classic nuclear family. My father knew best. My mother stayed at home. My brother's name wasn't Dick, it was Jack. He's four years older than I am, and Mother always told me he was smarter than I was, that I shouldn't be too smart, and I shouldn't work so hard or else I'd never get married. What I wanted more than anything was to be normal, not to be teased for being fat and smart, and not to be different. My father went away to war (World War II, dear), while all my friends' fathers stayed home and made money and all my friends' mothers hoarded pineapple juice. (My mother was a single parent for five years.) Now think about your family of origin. How many brothers and sisters did you have?

Unlike our grandparents' families, your family of origin was also possibly quite small. It depends on how old you are. Both my grandmothers bore seven children, six and five of each family surviving to adulthood. But if my parents were your grandparents' generation, then their families were probably smaller, like mine, because of the Great Depression. If you are a Baby Boomer, one of the 60 million people born in North America between 1946 and 1962, then you probably came from a family of three to five children. By contrast, your family of procreation is going to be (or is) considerably smaller – one or two children at most. And sometimes you can't help asking why. A no-frills kid today, we're told, costs about the price of a small house ($100,000) to raise to the age of eighteen. What is it all for?

The Family of Procreation

When people leave their families of origin and marry and raise families of their own they create the new families of procreation (which are the families of origin for their children). But they bring patterns and tapes from their families of origin to the new family of procreation. We used to say to my daughter Liz, "You should be a lawyer, you're so nit-picking." She isn't, but she acted as her own counsel for her divorce, and she reminded me then of what we said. (Actually, she's precise, like my aunt Alma.)

This is what R.D. Laing means when he speaks of the scripts we play out, carrying them from our family of origin into our family of procreation, where it starts all over again. Maybe it's too late (I hope not!) to learn how to prevent such prophecies from taking over our children's lives.

Apart from the prophecies, what about other expectations? The old tapes don't work any more. Some of the expectations of behaviour and performance are simply obsolete and have no relevance to what kids are facing today. We can't preach nineteenth-century morality to a hi-tech generation. So we have to find new guidelines and new ways to teach them, but in the meantime, let's agree that the family is a crucible, framing us, moulding us, for good or ill.

What Are Families For?

Following are comments from little kids about families, from Naomi Hample's *Hugging, Hitting, and Other Family Matters*:

"We need families because you can't be alone, except for grown-ups." *Suzy*
"Families are really for sharing love." *David*
"If there weren't no families there wouldn't be no kids." *Bill*

And best of all, as James says, "We need families because otherwise we would have no place to go." Before we get too maudlin, consider what Ugo Betti has to say about family: "I think the family is the place where the most ridiculous and least respectable things in the world go on."

What do you think?

Yes, yes, all of the above. This is what families have been in the past. But what's going to happen tomorrow? Times have changed, and so have families, and what you need are some crystal ball predictions and some practical tips, starting now!

CHAPTER TWO

Happily Ever After

It is only possible to live happily ever after on a day-to-day basis.
— *Margaret Bonnano*

Once upon a time, so the story goes, and it still goes on, there was a young woman – a stepdaughter, as it turned out, so she had some experience of blended families – who found herself spending too many nights staring into the fire and wondering why life was passing her by. It was not that she lived in a slow lane, but her talents were largely unrecognized and certainly unrewarded. She did for her stepmother and stepsisters all day long, and in a big house this was no easy matter, responding to their every beck and call. We'll call her Ms. C.

As luck would have it, one of those once-in-a-lifetime opportunities arose, not a lottery but close to it – a chance to win a prince of one's own. The king was going to hold a singles dance and let all the eligible maidens (women, that is) fight for their rights on the dance floor. All they needed, it seemed, was a pretty face and a new dress.

Ms. C's stepsibs and even her stepmother – a widow, after all, and therefore eligible – went off to the royal meat market, leaving the girl at home with her ashes and rags. She had one hope. She had a godmother who knew how to turn a sow's ear into a silk purse, among other things, and a pumpkin into a vehicle, if you can believe it. This kind lady set her up (actually the prince was set up, when you come to think of it), and Ms. C was able to go off to the ball, looking like a million. (Like a million other young, pretty girls who rely on their looks to attract a man. Is there any other way?)

There, across a crowded room, the prince saw a stranger who looked very fetching. So he fetched her a glass of wine and danced with her and she danced divinely, though he wondered how because she had the strangest shoes he had ever seen. They didn't bend, and he could see her feet right through them. If he didn't know better, he'd have sworn they were made of glass.

"Quit while you're ahead," her godmother always used to say, so Ms. C took off at midnight but dropped one of those stupid shoes – on purpose?

The young prince – we'll call him Mr. P – couldn't get this lovely stranger out of his mind. And that stupid glass shoe piqued his curiosity. He organized a search, and the rest is history.

Mr. P and Ms. C were married. Using the glass slipper as an example of his remarkable sleuthing powers, he started a private investigation agency, specializing in insurance scams and bankruptcy claims (he'd had a lot of experience with this, too, as the old king was impoverished). Ms. C put her knowledge of ashes to good use and started a cottage industry, making miniature glass slippers and glass wedding bells to sell in craft stores as precious keepsakes of those special moments.

And they had children. A new family was begun, and that's when they discovered what was lying in wait behind that ridiculous pumpkin and those silly glass slippers. Like you and me, Ms. C and Mr. P discovered what family is all about. Family is a process.

What Does a Family Do?

Here's what a family does:
• provides a safe, regular sexual outlet for most of its adult

members. (Remember Shaw's definition of marriage offering "maximum temptation with maximum opportunity"? Let's hear it for the marriage bed!)

- provides the nation with new citizens. (This may be a problem for Canada soon. We have to reproduce at a rate of 2.1 people to maintain the population. We're dropping to about 1.7, which doesn't make up for the death rate. By the year 2030, the population of Canada will be decreasing. Immigration, anyone?)

- provides the small new citizens with health care, education, indoctrination, socialization and a certain measure of security until they can fend for themselves.

- provides the basis of order within the larger community by setting examples of democratic (or patriarchal) government, and demonstrating the effectiveness of co-operative behaviour.

- enables but also motivates the individual and the group to survive.

- provides markets for the distribution of goods and (increasingly) services and therefore:

- provides the backbone of the economy (also the legs and the wings).

When such tasks are abstracted and put into general terms, they don't seem like anything the families you and I know are doing in their daily lives. I mean, we're all just trying to get along, aren't we? Like Ms. C and Mr. P, we're just trying to discover the secret of living happily ever after in the last decade of the twentieth century. It's not as easy as it used to be. (Though it never was.)

The question is, why didn't the fairy godmother slip a couple of books on marriage and the family into the seat cushions of the pumpkin? Poor Ms. C and Mr. P set about raising their children with no training or knowledge, worrying about the kids' shots and vitamins and nutrition, then about day care, schooling, physical development and education, and also about trust, affection, communication, and morality. I doubt that it ever entered Mr. P's or Ms. C's mind when they were dancing the night away at that divine ball.

Happy Families

Tolstoy said that all happy families are alike, but who ever said any family was happy? Family therapists are busy these days trying to keep families "healthy" – forget happy. Dixie Guldner, a Kitchener family therapist and counsellor, calls the healthy family process the "dance of connecting and standing alone." (That's not the same as dancing all night. We'll analyze the steps of the dance as we go along.) Jane Howard, in her book *Families*, lists ten qualities common to "good families," that is, "clans that stick together, glued by affection if not by physical proximity." Here they are (with comments):

- a distinguished member, a success, a founder – someone to emulate. (Somewhere in your wider circle of relatives you must have someone you're proud of!)
- a member who keeps track of the clan, facilitates communication between far-flung members and maintains the family scrapbooks and photo albums. (I call this person the archivist. On my mother's side of the family it's my cousin's wife; on my father's side there isn't anyone, so we are scattered and lost.)
- busy members, with parents and children devoted to outside pursuits as well as each other. (This is part of Guldner's "dance," connecting and standing alone.)
- hospitable homes, with friends and relatives warmly received, with all willing to lend aid and support in times of need. (If you doubt me, look at what happens when there's a funeral.)
- at least one cherished eccentric and a general tolerance for the failings of the various members. (What else would you have to talk about when you all get together?)
- fixed, prized rituals, both traditional, such as Christmas customs, and unique celebrations invented by the family (see rituals, page 131).
- affectionate touching, hugs and comforting. (Let's hear it for hugs!)
- a sense of place, if not a childhood home, then a collection of

familiar belongings that symbolize "home." (You must know, as I do, families who move a lot. They create home wherever they go with a small but beloved collection of things – paintings, perhaps, or a few special books, including scrapbooks of momentoes, anything that gives them a sense of continuity.)

- children, not necessarily blood-related, who are included in the talk and laughter.
- elders who are honoured, with the width of the age range corresponding with the strength of the tribe.

It reads like a recipe, doesn't it? Families, however, don't get put together like puddings. Not these days.

PART TWO

Work and Money

CHAPTER THREE

Double Income Families

At work you think of the children you've left at home. At home, you think of the work you've left unfinished. Such a struggle is unleashed, your heart is rent. — *Golda Meir*

The so-called nuclear family – bread-winning father, stay-at-home mother, 2.5 children – is almost obsolete. It now comprises only 4 to 7 percent (depending on who's counting) of the population. The chief differing qualifier is the stay-at-home mother. It seeems there are very few of them left. In 1950 about 15 percent of married women worked outside the home. By 1980 that figure had risen to 52 percent. The prediction is that by 1990, 75 percent of all mothers with children under ten years of age will be working outside the home. I'll tell you one thing: that's an awful lot of tired mothers!

In a majority of these families, the wife's income is necessary for survival, not merely for material goods or her sanity. Not only are costs higher but wages are lower. I know, I know, financial experts tell us that we work fewer hours now to buy a pair of shoes than we did in the thirties or whenever. But in the past only one person had to work to buy shoes for the whole family. Nowadays wages are not geared to support a family. So the wife has to work to help support the family and to raise her children in a style, I admit, to which my family was not accustomed.

Bottom line for a lot of people in North America is higher than it ever was; pleasures are not simple or cheap any more. Reformers who predicted a life of productive leisure for the worker once the forty- (or thirty-five-) hour week was established didn't realize how expensive leisure time was going to be. We have become a nation of consumers and hedonists, all wanting to live the good life. The good life costs: gourmet cooking with trendy foods, wine with dinner (not only for special, rare occasions), Sunday brunch, spectator sports, theatre performances, concerts, jogging, snow and water sports, photography, travel and appropriate clothes and equipment for all these activities. *Very* expensive.

A Day in the Life

What has happened to the leisure time that all this was supposed to be enjoyed in? The double-income family seems to be so busy earning the money for it that it doesn't have time to enjoy it. (I'm talking about families with children.) The day starts early, with finding clean clothes for everyone, packing lunches, driving little ones to day care, preparing for work. At the other end it's pick-up time, a few wash loads, something for dinner (and if someone forgot to thaw the meat, it's fast-food time: take-out or microwave), dishes, bathtime, story, TV or homework (for both adults and children), early exhaustion. Weekends are for errands, groceries, renovations, chauffeuring to hockey, swimming, ballet, baton practice. Have I mentioned the electronic baby-sitter? Yes, TV is in there, at once a boon and a bone of contention.

The wife and mother who works outside the home works an estimated sixty-hour week. She has actually cut her housework time from eight hours a day to five, but she is working a thirty-five- to forty-hour week elsewhere. The husband whose wife goes to work increases his share of the housework an average of four hours a week. The wife is suffering from a kind of madness: it's called overwork, also known as burnout. It seems to be an occupational hazard for any woman who tries to run a house and hold down a job at the same time. There aren't enough hours in the day. Something has to give. And a lot does.

Like the cleaning, bed-making, mending, a lot of the cooking, social life and volunteer work, story-time – and the children – sometimes get short-changed. "If only," wailed one mother, "I could send the children out with the shirts."

This is where quality time begins (and ends) in the Two-Job Juggle that most working mother-wives perform. Torn in at least three directions at once, such women know that something has to give and pray it isn't their own sanity, more likely to pop than panty hose and less easy to replace.

CHAPTER FOUR

How to Juggle Two Jobs at Once

I feel guilty when I'm staying at home and my associates are working. I feel guilty when I'm working and my child is in someone else's care.
— *Deborah Dubose,* from a *Newsweek* report, 1986

Men First

Men, of course, have their own juggling act to do. They also experience this home/work juggling routine, though not as often as women. I read a book about stay-at-home fathers, three different men who were rewarded by wonderful bonding (as they say) with their infants while their wives were the sole breadwinners (through special circumstances, and for a limited time). The book's introduction was taken up with the author's account of how difficult it had been to find her subjects. Similarly, it is difficult to find male single parents who are daily living out the real-life experiences of Kramer and Son. A man with very young children usually hires a housekeeper to cover his absence and his other household needs. (That's when he begins to discover what wives are worth on the wage scale.) A man with older children tends to be like the widowed Captain von Trapp (in *The Sound of Music*) who assigned tasks as if he were in the army and his children recalcitrant recruits. I venture to say that a married father with a job does not have to juggle as much as a wife does.

Having said that, I expect to receive an argument, and so I will try to refute it. I know a couple, the female half of which has to travel quite frequently during the week, and he manages admirably, getting their two preschool children up and fed and cleaned and off to day care, then picked up at the end of the day, fed, read to, tucked in. He can manage some basic grocery shopping, but the laundry and the housecleaning wait until his wife returns on the weekend. The youngest child, a little girl almost three, although docile and obedient enough during her mother's absences, tends to cling and demand a lot when her mother is home.

As a writer, I have known a number of men who are artists (writers, composers, visual artists) and work at home, or at least outside regular office hours and downtown places of employment. One of them was an effective house-husband, there to welcome the kids home for lunch, sign their notes, be on hand for after-school crises. He was very good at it. I know another one, with a studio a short walk from the house, who treats his job like a punch-the-clock affair and walks away from the household and child-care responsibilities. I know a couple of divorced writer-fathers who have divided their children and their obligations with whichever wife mothered various of the children. The kids, fortunately, are older and can do a little fending for themselves. Each of these cases seems to me special and is treated as such. No general rules can be drawn from them.

How Do You Juggle Two Jobs at Once?

So we come back to you – probably female, probably harassed, probably clutching at straws to find more energy, more efficiency and less guilt in the superhuman task you face of being wife, mother and worker in a day that has only twenty-four hours in it. The women's magazines that address the two-job problem often succeed in making you feel more guilty because *no one* can be that organized or that calm. That's fiction; out here is reality, and it has to be lived daily.

Men suffer from the pressure, too, but have different pressure and weak points. Lots of men now cook, but most of them still forget the vegetables. They seem to have a higher tolerance level for dirt, but a lot of them like things to be neat. They spend more time than their fathers did playing with their children, but they still aren't very good about distractions and noise. Most of them are happy to have their wives work when it comes to that second paycheque, but they still aren't willing to spend as much time on the housework to help her. The key word is *help*, instead of *share*. Housework and child care are still considered the wife's responsibility, whether or not she works outside the home. What is necessary is a summit conference. If you haven't yet had one (or several), now is the time.

Summit Conference

First things first. The same question can be applied to your job, your family and your self as has to be applied to money and the dispersal of it. We're talking about time, after all. So ask yourself: What is your time worth? When you can honestly answer that question, you have the answer to a lot of your other problems. Because it is possible to buy some of the solutions.

- Outside cleaning help. While you're looking around for someone to become an interested friend of the family, who cleans your cupboards without being asked and brings you home-made soup, don't ignore the rental maid services. Their staff are bonded and trained, and you can complain if they miss something, whereas with the old-fashioned cleaning lady, you have to put up with her weaknesses. Most working couples sooner or later need someone to come in and shovel out the place on a regular basis. They usually find it worth the expense, since it keeps down the resentment as well as the dirt.
- The next thing you have to decide is how much help do you need? Some couples do well with once or twice a month

cleaning, but the help is habit-forming, and they soon find it convenient to have it once a week. It depends on your dirt-threshold as well as your finances.

- Who's going to pick up? Apart from the dirt, there's the tidying. It should not be one person's job. Assign family members individual responsibilities and see that they perform. It can be one room per person, or the newspapers and the magazines for one, wastebaskets for another, dirty dishes and glasses (they do spread over a house) for another. Lillian Gilbreth in her invaluable book *Management in the Home* tells you how to assign tasks, with job descriptions, breakdown of jobs and so on. These can be used for daily and weekly chores as well as for regular or annual events.
- Just as with other rules (see page 55), there have to be consequences if the jobs are not performed. If necessary, go on strike.
- But you don't want a mutiny on your hands. So decide what your tolerance level is. How much mess can you stand? How often do you want to look with satisfacton at a clean, tidy house? I know one short-sighted, happy woman who simply takes off her glasses when the dust gets too thick.
- Make sure you're not house-proud and house-poor. Some people are breaking their necks paying for a house that simply doesn't suit their lifestyle. You may want to relax your goals as well as your standards. In the case of a major decision like this – where and how to live – make sure you both agree.
- If you don't agree, well, that's the reason for the summit conference, isn't it? When both partners work, both should have some say in their living decisions. I read somewhere that a wife's decision-making power goes up with every $1,000 she makes. Where does that leave the low-income woman? Wives still perform services that can't be priced. Make sure your services are acknowledged at decision time.
- Both parties, by the way, are entitled to some time off. It's estimated that a stay-at-home mother has about thirty-five hours a week leisure time, a working wife about twenty-five hours, and a working husband about fifty. A fairer dispersal of time would go a long way to solving some of the

household management problems that women seem to encounter more often than men.

Time, you see, is money in a different form.

Getting Organized

Sometimes the problems can be solved without resorting to a major philosophical confrontation simply by getting organized. Some organizing involves some initial costs, but they may be worth it if they resolve a conflict. For instance:

- It costs money to buy a duvet – or several of them. But once you have them, you never have to make a bed again. A flick every morning means a neat bed – or several of them.
- Colour-coded bed linen means instant recognition and allocation.
- Ditto towels.
- A roll of paper towelling installed under the bathroom sink(s), and maybe a large sign until people get trained, means everyone cleans the basin and tub after use. (The toilet is negotiable.)
- Paper-cup dispensers in bathroom and kitchen mean not only superior hygiene but fewer glasses to wash or to clutter up a counter.
- I'm as ecological as the next person, and since the last few suggestions have been filling too many landfill sites, why not use napkin rings and cloth napkins instead of paper serviettes and wash them once a week (unless you had spaghetti)?
- Practise preventive housecleaning at all times and stop dirt before it happens – at the door with lots of space for muddy boots, wet coats, mitts, umbrellas, whatever; in the kitchen with foil element and oven drip-catchers, easy-spray cleaners and cleaning cloths; and anywhere in the house with a hard-line policy about clean-as-you-go.
- In the summer and on weekends try tray lunches, very good for using up leftovers: dibs and dabs of finger salad ingredients, sandwich fillings, bread, cheese, and so on, with individual baskets instead of plates to save on clean-up.

Many time-saving ideas may initially cost some money but

once established will give you back a greater return. The best thing about being organized is that you feel you're in charge. You are in control of your life and not letting it run you.

But What About the Children?

You can't give the children a shake as you do a duvet and expect them to lie there neat and tidy until you're ready for them. All the books (and all the common sense) in the world keep reminding us that children won't wait. In one way, that's very positive. Since they won't wait, you must deal with them when the need arises – like every day – and that's good for both of you. It's nice to be with people you love. On the other hand, because they won't wait, if you don't do something about them, someone or something else will, and you might not like the results.

I'll go into detail about communication and listening later, both very necessary skills to practise with one's children. As for the care and feeding of husbands, we'll deal with them generally under marriage: sex, companionship, and so on. A lot of what we're talking about has to do with personal happiness and enthusiasm. I'll discuss happiness later, too, but right here is the best place to consider meaningful activity. If you really like what you're doing and are convinced of its and your value, then you're halfway there.

For years I've been telling widows first, then singles of every ilk, to have a reason to get out of bed every morning. I guess it really applies to everyone. If you're involved, vitally involved, in doing things that fulfill you as a person, that express what you believe your life to be about, then you're on the road to happiness with your family. Dusting, folding laundry, picking up the groceries, cutting someone's hair or toenails, scraping plasticine off a knife, wiping up someone's spilled milk, blowing up balloons, fixing a doll's eyes, bandaging a cut, reading Three Billy Goats Gruff for the forty-seventh time, sewing a costume for a school play, sponging someone's feverish head – I could go on and on, and so could you, and you will. All these activities are daily acts of love that go with the job. There's room in all of them for joy.

And that's how you keep juggling, because you know why.

How to Make Yourself Miserable

Paul Dickson's *The Official Rules* lists ten instructions on how to be miserable. If you want to forget the juggling act and spiral into despair, follow these rules:

- Forget the good things in life and concentrate on the bad.
- Put an excessive value on money.
- Think that you are indispensable to your job, your community and your friends. (That means giving the lowest priority to your family.)
- Think that you are overburdened with work and that people tend to take advantage of you.
- Think that you are exceptional and entitled to special privileges.
- Think that you can control your nervous system by sheer willpower.
- Forget the feelings and rights of other people.
- Cultivate a consistently pessimistic outlook.
- Never overlook a slight or forget a grudge.
- And don't forget to feel sorry for yourself.

If that doesn't make you feel overworked, underappreciated, helpless, hopeless, desperate and miserable, nothing will.

CHAPTER FIVE

The Stay-at-Home Mother

It is impossible for any woman to love her children twenty-four hours a day. — *Milton R. Sapirstein*

The Mad Housewife

Does anyone remember Sue Kaufman's novel *Diary of a Mad Housewife*? (Mad herself, bless her, Kaufman jumped off a building a few years after she published that and another novel, *Falling Bodies*.) It was my generation of mothers she was writing about – us, me. Mine is the generation that became addicted to Valium as doctors tried to keep us pacified in our domestic cages. (I never took it.) Mine is the generation that Betty Friedan wrote *The Feminine Mystique* for in 1963. (From the moment I read that book, I never made a bed again, except once a week to change the sheets.)

For some of us it was too late. Some of my peers had such a vested interest in their lives they couldn't afford to change. Change would have made a mockery of what they had put their life's effort into. Their children have grown up now, so they're not mad any more. Some of them, however, are angry because they have become victims of the mid-life dump, but that's another story.

It's a new generation and a new problem now. Working wives and mothers are the norm, and it takes a conscious decision to stay at home. There is usually a prescribed time limit: perhaps only the length of a maternity leave, or for the toddler years, or, at most, "just until the children start school." Even when a mother does stay at home for a time, it's with the clear understanding that she will return to work.

Why Did They Leave?

Betty Friedan and *The Feminine Mystique* got the blame, but Barbara Ehrenreich (*The Hearts of Men*) claims that the philosophy according to *Playboy* (1957) was responsible for women leaving the kitchen. Hugh Hefner told men it was okay to be a swinger, that it was neither irresponsible nor immoral to stay (or return to being) single and to stop footing the bill for stay-at-home mothers. According to statistics, a lot of wives and mothers were working outside the home before that, out of financial necessity. (Diehards still refuse to recognize the feminist movement as an economic one.) Anyway, as we all know by now, the percentage of women in the work force, whether they're singles or wives, mothers or not, has risen enormously in the last twenty-five years. The expectation for any woman now, no matter what her personal circumstances, is that she will spend thirty to forty-five years of her life in the labour force.

Work outside the home is not only necessary (and accepted) for most women, it is also expected. Whereas in the fifties the woman who worked was looked down on for neglecting her husband, children and home, the woman in the seventies was regarded as a sloven and a parasite if she stayed home and looked after the children while her husband did all the work. (At the same time, women who were trying to do it all kept reminding their husbands that housework didn't get done all by itself and children couldn't be put on hold like a demanding client.) There has remained a hard core of women who settled for less (financially) and stayed at home to look after the kids. They're part of that 4 to 7 percent who make up the nuclear family. Now some of the so-called Superwomen envy them, so much so that some of them are deciding to stay at home – at least for a while. Now that the Big Boom generation is into children, some of the Boom parents are deciding they want to give their children what they had: cookies after school and someone there to listen. Maybe that's what husbands want, too.

Only a Housewife

A taxi driver I talked to told me his wife had never worked, even after the kids were grown. "When women go out, they find another man," he said and told me about a friend of his that happened to. Better, he felt, to suffer a little financially and keep the wife at home waiting for him. He still managed to take her home to Greece every year. (There are times I think I'm in the wrong business.) Middle-class husbands don't feel quite the same. They like the income a career wife brings in. At the same time they miss home-baked cookies and hand-ironed shirts like mom used to provide. Catch-22. "Just a housewife" may be easy to put down, but it hurts to lose her services.

The wife sees it differently. By staying at home she eases both that terrible guilt she feels every day about neglecting her children and the bone-weariness of trying to handle two (or more) jobs. Tillie Olsen put it memorably in her classic award-winning story, "I Stand Here Ironing":

"I did not know then what I know now — the fatigue of the long day, and the lacerations of group life in nurseries that are only parking places for children."

It's hard to juggle one child, husband and job, but it can be done. With two or more children it gets tougher. Time, time is the killer. There's never enough of it, never enough to go around, to get everything done, keep everyone happy, and still get enough rest. So it is increasingly tempting to take some time off and be a full-time mother, give the children a good start. Women are consciously making this choice now, not in huge numbers, but in numbers large enough to constitute a vanguard, a trend that is being recognized in the women's magazines.

You know what happens? Guilt is replaced not only by apologies but also – worse – by loneliness and a desperate feeling of isolation. We're back to the fifties mother coping with all her pent-up intelligence with the little minds in her care and all the mindless, repetitive home duties that could, if one were working on the outside, be justifiably disregarded or left to the not-so-thorough attentions of a rental maid. Only this time round there isn't any company.

Coffee, Anyone?

New stay-at-home mothers tell me they are too scattered and isolated now to do each other any good. "I may be home," one told me, "but the mother next door isn't." She hasn't anyone to go to the playground with her and her kids because her neighbours' children are in day care all day.

One young woman opted to stay home with her first child and gave day care to her baby's two cousins, one older, one younger, the children of her two sisters-in-law. (Well, not gave – they paid her.) Another woman runs a little nursery school for two same-age friends of her preschool children, also for pay. This is a neat compromise: staying home, still earning some money, and providing one's children with companions. What I and my contemporaries did on a part-time basis, taking turns to be block hostess and bartering baby-sitting services, has turned into yet another cottage industry. Why weren't we that smart?

But for those mothers who don't turn a penny on home-care, and even for those who do, loneliness (for adult company) and the full burden of responsibility can weigh heavy. And one's former peers (that is, women who are still working) are asking whatever do you do all day, and how can you stand it, vegetating like that, and isn't it time you pulled your own weight? It's the flip side of the guilt-edged coin. If mothers work full-time outside the house they feel guilty about neglecting their kids; they feel guilty about their husband having to shoulder the financial burden all by himself if they don't. Nevertheless, the idea of staying at home with the children, for a few years at least, for their formative years, is gradually becoming more acceptable.

The Cost

Financial sacrifice is involved, but to some extent it is balanced by the savings: no child-care expenses, fewer clothes, perhaps only one car, lower food costs (frugal cooking takes time). One young woman who tried it both ways and went back to work in spite of the higher costs (most of her salary goes for child care), sums up the hidden costs for a lot of women: "I went stir-crazy. Here at work I feel fulfilled."

There are other, more serious, long-term costs implicit in staying home. SAHs may lose pension benefits built up prior to departure from business. Professional sacrifices may be involved as well, and though intangible, they are harder to recover from. A woman with a demanding career may slip badly in the five to eight years she stays at home. She loses currency in her field as well as advancement. It may take some time for her to catch up, if she ever will, when she returns. A lot of careers won't wait.

But neither will children. They grow up all too quickly. I know women with time-bomb careers (that is, their age and appearance are factors in their success – as in the performing arts) who have to make a hard choice between staying at home and enjoying their children's formative years or continuing to pursue a career while their own youth is still marketable.

Either/Or

Alice Walker wrote: "Someone asked me once whether I thought women artists should have children, and since we were beyond discussing why this question is never asked of artists who are men, I gave my answer promptly. 'Only one . . . Because with one you can move . . . With more than one you're a sitting duck.' " This, of course, is one of the major reasons why dedicated career women choose to remain childless, or to have only one child. All women, artists or not, face this terrible either/or choice that life seems to demand of them, especially of stay-at-home women.

That's not quite true. The choice is there for everyone; stay-at-home mothers are simply more conscious of it. They're also aware that no either/or choice is permanent. It took me a long time to learn that. I used to say to myself, "Today is not forever; it only feels like it."

Most stay-at-home mothers intend to go back to work, at least part-time. A lot of stay-at-home mothers, in fact, work part time, but the work is a low priority compared to their other tasks and goals. In addition to the benefits they feel their choice gives their families, most stay-at-home mothers regard their mothering sabbatical as a valuable assessment time.

Some Case Histories

I know one woman who took time off from her teaching career to stay home with her children. When she ventured out again, she went into television. Learning while she earned her new living, she is now an award-winning producer of educational films. I know another woman who left full-time employment in the publishing industry to become a part-time editor to allow her to spend more time with her young family. Now, busier as her children grow older, she can call her own shots, juggling time for illnesses or birthday parties or vacations and still making a good living. (Her husband does most of the cooking.) She's my favourite editor.

Some women share jobs as a means of hanging on to the best of both worlds. I read of one young woman who, after her son was born, began sharing a position as a human-resource specialist. She works two and a half days a week for half salary and full benefits (a rare and privileged case). If you have a saleable skill that's in demand, it's easier to bargain for such a deal. If not, then you may do what many women have done – create your own job.

Two young mothers designed snow-proof, child-manage-able snowsuits (with wonderful storm cuffs, Velcro fastenings, double collars, and so on) and peddled them to retailers out of their basements, spelling each other off on selling trips and handling the books on their dining room tables with the help of two co-operative husbands. You read of women who parlay their grandmother's cookie recipes into a mega-business, set up exercise classes for pregnant mothers, package and sell gift baskets for all occasions, and don't forget our Ms. C and her glass ornaments. The list goes on and on, of women who see a need and fill it, for money, in their spare time. Sometimes, it seems, for part-time stay-at-homes, either/or can be both.

Who's the Best?

So who's the best mother: Superwoman, Stay-at-Home, or Part-Time? The question can't be answered in quantitative terms of time or of money. Money and success, the esteem of one's peers, elapsed time in the house, skill at the balancing act – none of these really provides an answer. The proof, the saying goes, is in the pudding, in this case in the children. You can't fault full-time career wives and dismiss their children as victims of neglect.

Stay-at-home mothers often do more for their children than is necessary or useful to their development. The children are often helpless and ungrateful and remember mom as Mother Drudge. On the other hand, SAHs can be awfully busy, too. Many of them, to prevent mental stagnation or to keep some currency with the outside world, take courses or do volunteer work that can threaten to take over all their time. (In my day there were big-time volunteer organizers who, it was said, could run General Motors if asked. The only difference between them and their high-powered executive husbands was that they weren't being paid for their work.)

In any case, there are other ways of being busy than being employed outside the home. Just because a body is physically present doesn't mean the child has her full attention. "Not now, dear, I'm busy" can be heard from Stay-at-Home Mom as well as Superwoman. Is mere presence enough? Guilty working mothers sometimes think so. Stay-at-home mothers know it takes more than being an in-house washing machine to qualify as an important presence in their children's lives.

But who can define the feeling of security a child has knowing that mom's home? Are we going to get maudlin about cookies in the oven? Surveys reveal high qualities of independence, self-reliance, self-esteem, maturity and responsibility among children of working mothers (see working children, page 68). On the other hand, if mother is working outside the home, that means someone else is caring for the children. It depends on the age of the child, of course, as well as on the quality of the care-giver, whether this is a good or a bad thing.

I Remember Mama

Here's an interesting exercise: take some time to unreel your mind and seek out your earliest memory. What is it? Examine it carefully and see if you can spread out a little from that drop of memory, finding whose face surfaces from the pool of your past. This exercise, conducted by a team of researchers reporting in *Psychology Today*, disclosed in older subjects a first conscious memory associated with their mothers. Younger people, whose mothers, perhaps working, were away from home more had fewer early memories of their female parent. A child's first mirror is its primary care-giver. What images is it receiving? (Infants are at highest risk for physical reasons as well. The exchange of germs is rampant in the day-care nurseries of North America. G.I. – for Gastro-Intestinal disturbances – could be every infant's middle initials.)

They say the returns won't be in for another generation at least. And whatever you do today, your children will do differently tomorrow, to show you how it should be done. This is the meaning of progress, I suppose: it skips a generation. Whatever happens in the future, at least there is some growing respect for the stay-at-home mother. Her choice is acknowledged as a valid one among many. There is still, however, no monetary value put on her choice. It penalizes her financially and socially. We still tend to glorify professionals. At least, we pay them.

CHAPTER SIX

How to Decide about Money

One of the pleasantest things in married life is that you have no money of your own, but have to come to your husband for every sixpence.
— *M.V. Hughes, A London Girl of the 1880s*

The Value of a Family

The family, we seldom stop to realize, is one of the major economic units of society today. It's no longer the major producing unit, as it once was, but it is still a consuming unit. It still controls the reproduction of human beings (despite the efforts of test-tube fathers), still provides the first training in language and cultural behaviour and basic education and life skills. It is the moral and social arbiter of a nation and also the psychological barometer. Being the foundation upon which we build everything else (that is, public appearance, behaviour, lifestyle, culture, morality and values), it is beneath conscious recognition most of the time. It is also beyond price.

That doesn't stop some people from trying to price it. The argument goes on, for example, generation after generation, as to how much a homemaker is worth, and her unpaid services keep going up in estimate if not in estimation. Now the money experts are putting a price tag on children. It costs, they say, $100,000 to raise a no-frills child to the age of eighteen – so that doesn't count postsecondary education. And then they ask, is it worth it?

It's not if, as Robert Glossop of the Vanier Institute of the Family charges, you insist on putting price tags on people. Price-tag mentalities are not new, but they're still scary, especially when applied to human values, which can't be bought though they can be paid for. The family is still our main life-support system, and it costs more than money to maintain.

Surveys have revealed that people without children can give you at least eight good reasons why they don't have them; people with children can't think of one good reason for having them – yet they go on raising them and loving them. Well, of course, everything is relative. The average house now costs about $100,000, and a kid is worth as much as a house, or don't you agree?

The point is, do you know where your money is? For there, also, may be your heart.

A Premarital Money Talk

If you didn't have this conversation before you were married, you can have it now. Sharpen your pencils and allow some time for it.

• Make a list of what you own and what you owe. Figure out what you want to keep separate and what you want to share. It's called separate bank accounts: his, hers and ours.

• Do you want to add your spouse's name to the lease on your apartment or the deed to your house or condo? Do you know what joint ownership involves in the event of your divorce or death? What happens to your half? What about your children, if any?

• What about car(s)? Paintings? Jewellery? Furs? Collections? Anything of value, or that you care enough about to worry what's going to happen to it if anything happens to you?

• Check your insurance policies and maybe work out some new arrangements. Look at the group insurance provided by each place of business (assuming you both work) and decide whether one of you will take the spousal benefits of the other's policy, if possible. Then the other's insurance might be converted to something else.

- Don't forget disability insurance. And what about your medical insurance? Compare the benefits and maybe drop one. Does anyone have dental insurance?
- What about death benefits? Some companies still provide aid to a man if his spouse dies but not to a woman if she is bereaved. Find out.
- Plan to take any legitimate tax deductions off the higher income, if possible, to lower the tax.
- Do you each have a will? If not, make one; if so, update it. It's a mess if either of you dies without one.
- Decide ahead of time, before you get into a specific fight, how much you plan to save each year. Do your goals match? (This is much more important than matching sheets and towels.) If you are saving for a holiday, a house, retirement, you might set up a joint savings account (or investment) with that goal in mind, and each of you contribute an agreed-upon amount monthly.

Double Income Families

Dinks (Double Income No Kids) don't have many problems. They and their affluent peers, the unattached singles, are the ones the up-tempo markets cater to. The life of conspicuous consumption goes on. Someone has to buy all those Calvin Klein clothes, the chocolate-flavoured pasta (served with a melted ice cream - rum sauce) and the cellular phone to keep in touch with their brokers (especially these days!). ("There must be more to life than having everything," said Maurice Sendak.)

When Dinks have kids, they become Yuppies (odious term), and their 1.7 (or less) children are the ones who wear the kiddies' designer clothes and who drop lines I wouldn't believe if I hadn't heard them myself:

"Such a pretty blouse!" I said, unsuspecting. "Where did you get it?"

"France, of course," was the blasé answer from a nine-year-old.

"I love the milkshakes in Helsinki," said a ten-year-old, contributing to an adult conversation about travel.

"How can I get a good glaze on my pottery if I don't have my own kiln?" asked an eleven-year-old.

"I can handle my own crêpes," said a ten-year-old when I offered to make pancakes for him.

And I had thought my own child was precocious in her time when she complained, at age nine, "How is it that every time we have artichokes we have Cherries Jubilee?" I, too, contributed to that consumerism that overtakes families and threatens to inundate them with desires masked as needs.

Double income families are the ones that have rendered the nuclear family almost obsolete, for both husband and wife work outside the home. You have to consider the sheer logistics of it – the handling of time, the juggling of tasks and children, coping with stress, all that. But one of the major considerations is money. You have a few decisions to make before you throw yourself in front of the wheel of fortune, some of which I have already listed. Do both incomes go into one kitty? Is there an agreement as to who pays for what? In the event of a split, who gets what, and is the division fair? No one – least of all husbands and wives – can afford to be naive or dewy-eyed about money any more.

We all know the Queen doesn't carry money (don't you ever wonder what's in that ubiquitous handbag hanging on her arm?), and very rich men don't because a wallet puts an unsightly bulge in their handmade Italian silk suits. The rest of us plebs carry cash, at least one credit card and three or four other pieces of identification to testify to our ability to pay our bills, plus glasses, dark and bi- for some, cigarettes for those who still indulge, makeup, however basic, and other items too numerous and personal to mention.

You've come a long way, baby, but not nearly long enough. There are still wives who have no discretionary money of their own, who have no sense of money, though they may be a whiz with the household accounts, but who are, as the National Council of Women puts it, "one man away from welfare." I can't begin to offer advice about budgets, savings, investments, mortgages, insurance, pensions, annuities, RRSPs, RRIFs and so on in one tiny section of a book about the family. (Let me refer you to *Everywoman's Money Book* by Lynne MacFarlane and me.) I can offer a few general but cogent observations and some sweeping conclusions (I'm good at sweeping).

A Little Consciousness-Raising

All we can do with money in this book is talk about your basic attitudes both to it and to your control of it. I recommend that anyone who wants to live with someone else maintain a separate bank account in addition to the joint one. Certainly it's convenient and trusting to have a joint account, but everyone is entitled to discretionary money.

Lynne MacFarlane and I tell all those who will listen (and even those who don't) that they must save at least 10 percent of their income. (No matter what you may think, this *is* possible.) This applies to housewives, too, even those who must come to their husband for every sixpence. My message meets a lot of disbelief and resistance among the Stay-at-Homes, but I keep on saying it. Take a sugar bowl or a tin box and put all your quarters in it, for starters. Consider it a small salary for services rendered.

Who's Worth More?

Now, what about those services rendered? It has been noted, and not only by me, that when both parents work, the one with the lower income is the one on deck in the event of an emergency – child's illness, special event, whatever. Since women earn only 60 to 64 percent of what men earn, the wife/mother is usually the one on call. In the case of any decision involving a certain amount of personal sacrifice, time or effort, the nasty question often arises: How much is your time worth? (When it boils down to what Gloria Steinem calls "shitwork," that is, housecleaning/keeping, it often saves friction and feelings to hire a cleaning person rather than argue over the division of labour.)

Surveys indicate that a woman's chance of divorce increases with every $1,000 a month she earns. This is not the threat to uppity women that it might appear. The statistic doesn't say which spouse opts out; more frequently at this level it's the woman, because she has the financial ability to do so.

It's important to determine your attitude to money and to its source. Some working wives who used to stay home figure that what's yours is mine and what's mine is also mine. On the other hand, some husbands figure that what's mine is mine and what you make is also mine – and that, in fact, is the way it used to be when women were not allowed to own property in their own names. So you have to stop and decide who owns what, if anything.

Yours, Mine, Ours

Some double income families prefer to put everything into one big pot and pay for their expenses and desires from that; others will break down their dispersal of monies in other ways. In some families I know, the man's income pays for shelter, food, clothes, insurance and medical expenses (the basics) while the woman's money buys the extras: vacations, children's camps and special lessons and so on. I know of one husband who had a deal like that and who, when he split, took everything he had paid for – the house and contents. That was before the new family laws and divorce settlements (which are still inequitable, for other reasons).

As for the joint account and joint expenses, even if you don't draw up a marriage contract, it's wise for double income teams to come to some agreement as to the dispersal of monies, and not only who pays for what but who gets what's left over. (Dreamer!) It is also wise to be sure you agree on your goals. If both halves say yes, you would like to buy a house, but one or the other half persists in buying sports equipment, or clothes, or expensive dinners out, or VCRs, or CDs, so that the savings plan is sabotaged, then you'll have to go back to the budget plan and work it out again. Your needs, wants, must-haves, secret desires, priorities and attitudes change over the years, depending on your circumstances, children and-dare I say?-maturity. It would be nice if both of you grew up at the same rate, but it doesn't always happen. (That's when your very own account becomes indispensable.)

Into Every Life a Budget Must Fall

Having established your basic philosophy to money, you can then go on and work out a budget. Sharpen your pencil, and if you don't feel like making up your own lists, find a ready-made one (insurance and investment companies give them out for free; there's one in *Everywoman's Money Book*) and figure out your total income and expenses. Once you see where the money is going, you can begin to redirect it. Work out a practical budget you can both live by, and then live by it. The basic rule, I repeat, about savings is: save 10 percent of your gross income. Both of you.

Keep a little to yourself, even apart from your personal bank account, which is still sometimes accountable. You each need mad money, discretionary money of your own. You decide.

Children and Money

While you're deciding, you're giving a subliminal lesson about money to your children. Just as with sex, your attitudes will be apparent without your ever saying a word. It's better if you can talk about it (both sex and money). Kids learn the value of money by learning the value of *your* money - *your* value of money. Here are a few basic ideas that children can absorb in a family:

- Money doesn't grow on trees. Whether you can afford it or not, hand-outs should not be encouraged.
- All children are entitled to some discretionary money, that is, a basic allowance, geared to the age of the child, to spend as they please but not dependent on performance.
- Even very young children can earn extra money by doing household chores above and beyond the basic duties required of everyone. One family keeps a list of optional jobs on the fridge door with a wage attached to them. The kids

negotiate for the jobs and earn extra money doing them. It can be argued that this creates a mercenary attitude in children who do extra chores for money not for love. (In my day, the joke goes, I was good for nothing.) To counteract this tendency it helps to be properly grateful and to acknowledge service with a smile: a cup of tea brought to a resting parent, a swift errand run for a tired one, the first dandelion or pussy willow shared (this is getting close to ritual), a cartoon clipped for the family bulletin fridge. No one has put a price tag on these gestures (yet).

- Honesty is the best policy. If your children see that you don't cheat or chisel (not telling a clerk who has made a mistake with the change in your favour, taking equipment or supplies from your place of work, and so on), then they have a good example to follow – and vice versa.
- Help them to budget for realizable goals. And when a goal has been achieved, like enough money for a Walkman or some type of electronic equipment, teach them to shop carefully and compare values to get the most for their money.
- You might teach them the value of other things besides money and goods, but that's a whole other book.

I talk to a lot of people about money, and I find people's attitudes to money fascinating. The big U.S. money-book lady, Sylvia Porter, has commented that as a society we are spending fewer and fewer of our dollars on real goods and more and more on services, reflecting our hopes and wishes and image of ourselves, rather than our needs. I have already pointed out that families are no longer the producing unit of society: the family no longer sees to its own food production, brewing and baking, clothes manufacturing (nor all of its cleaning), equipment, soap or candle supplies – unless, in this strangely textural, dilettante society of ours, for aesthetic reasons.

I do know people who bake their own sourdough or triticale bread, who brew their own beer (my son, for one), make their own wine, sew their own clothes, fire their own pots and wine goblets, craft their own macramé wall-hangings, wooden bowls, beeswax candles, rose-petal pot pourris. Nevertheless. . .

Thomas Edison predicted that electricity would one day be so cheap that only the rich could afford candles. Have you looked at the price of hand-dipped, scented candles recently? We have turned our stores into temples of consumerism, elegant boutiques and esoteric shoppes where may be purchased – on credit, no money down – the wonders of the world, and even some of the curiosities, freaks and monstrosities that you never thought you needed until now. In addition to things, we may also buy sensations and experiences, everything from foods and the cooking thereof, musical and dramatic productions, adventure trips, cruises, safaris and treks, to simulated life events including surrogate lovers, factitious murders and porno-snuff films. And then there are holding tanks for total sensory deprivation; it costs to buy nothingness. None of these things costs as much as to raise a child, unless you become addicted. Addiction costs the most of all, addiction to anything, besides the better-known addictive substances.

The family, you see, is up against terrific competition, fighting for its dollars. People keep on making choices. Not as many are choosing children as used to. Quite a few who have children thrust upon them, as it were, are choosing negatively before (abortion) or after (divorce and custody given to the other parent) the fact. The birth rate is dropping, and by the next century – not so far away now – we will be facing a dwindling population. That, of course, will have its own economic effect. Since the family is one of the main economic units of society, obviously, as the family decreases in size, sustaining the economy will become increasingly difficult. Growth and production are dependent on the home market. If the home market declines, then so does the entire economy. Even divorce, which produces two households where there was one and which therefore requires duplication of equipment (beds, stoves, stereos and so on), won't help.

Everything gets political these days. We started out to have a little chat about family finances and look where we ended. Actually, we've only just begun.

PART THREE

Children

CHAPTER SEVEN

Child-Rearing

The best thing a father can do for his children is love their mother.
— *Reverend Hesburgh*

The Post-Hypnotic Trance

Psychiatrist R.D. Laing says we live our adult lives in a state of post-hypnotic trance left over from our childhoods. Most people never come out of the trance; if they do, it's quite painful. Laing's idea is that everyone in a family is given a scenario and assigned a role. The family, he thinks, is "a shared fantasy image . . . a container of some kind" (a nest?), an image "for which all members . . . may feel each should sacrifice themselves." He thinks that patterns are spread over generations and that we are acting parts that we have never read or seen but that are somehow there for us to play.

This kind of indoctrination in a different context has come to be called brainwashing. It goes on in every family. You hear people in families saying, "He's careful, like his uncle Harry." Or, "That boy will never amount to anything, he's so wild." Or, "Isn't she a little mother?" Or, "You're just like your crazy Aunt Suzy, taking in every stray that comes along."

You hear of young women marrying their fathers in the strong older men they think will take care of them, and of young men marrying their mothers for their comforting (young) bodies and uncritical minds. A daughter becomes the son her father never had; a boy becomes the mama's boy his prematurely widowed mother leans on until he bends.

Scripts People Play

This, I think, is what Laing means when he speaks of the scripts we play out and of the post-hypnotic state we all walk through for the rest of our lives, acting on the suggestions made to us in our childhood. It's not such a startling idea to us now. There's a whole related school of self-help based on the work of Eric Berne (*Games People Play*), examining the roles and scripts we have been forced into, perhaps against our will, more likely without our awareness. The antidote, the way to break out of this post-hypnotic state, is to *see* the knots we have been tied into or have tied ourselves into. By becoming aware of them, we have a chance of breaking out of the trap of self-fulfilling prophecy.

I hope it's not too late for us to know how to prevent such prophecies from taking over our children's lives. It would seem that the family of origin is a crucible, forming us, moulding us, for good or ill. Laing says it's a slaughter-house. Sociologist Erving Goffman says it's a Siberia. Are we talking about the North American family? It doesn't sound like "Father Knows Best," or even "Family Ties," whose major difference from the earlier TV show appears to be that both husband and wife work. What's happening to the children in the family?

Basic Approach

As in everything else, there are fashions in child-raising. My mother's generation believed in bottle-feeding babies strictly by the clock; my generation of mothers believed in the best of all permissive worlds according to Spock; my children's generation brings the New Father into the delivery room, puts the Snugli firmly onto his front and hopes to raise children with sweet reason.

Where once psychologists told mothers to go ahead and make strict rules, they went on to question the behaviour of both mother and child and put us in a double bind, which they then began to question. By the seventies, realizing women's lack of power, the experts were looking around to see who was giving the power to the kids (playing out their roles, inherited from Grandiose Grandma or Pontificating Pa?). Now they're onto family therapy, looking at the triangle, that is, dealing with mother, father and child within the family situation. If you start to analyze that, it's depressing. If the way you think and behave and respond is the end result of your particular situation and relationships rather than your situation and relationships being the result of your behaviour and beliefs, then you can't change without motivating the people around you to change as well. It would seem that no one does anything of one's own volition. We're all knee jerks, reacting to someone else's little hammer. It's especially humiliating if the hammer is in the hands of the child (and sometimes it is!), and it doesn't do anyone much good.

For example, a child can have enormous power in a stepfamily, enough in some cases to destroy the marriage. But disturbed power relationships can also happen in first-time families and destroy the children, or at least make a lot of people very unhappy. The omnipotent child is not a happy kid, wherever she is.

It's good for kids to have someone decide for them, up to a point. They get to that point and past it soon enough, and they'll let you know when, in no uncertain terms. But before it comes, you have to lay down the rules. Later, as the rules are reassessed and negotiated, you can offer guidance, which may or may not be accepted. You have to realize early on that certain areas of activity and behaviour – your child's safety, health, responsibility and basic morality – are not negotiable. You therefore do not allow them to be negotiated or even thought to be open to negotiation.

Thus, bedtime for a young child is not negotiable, because a child needs a certain number of hours of sleep (some less than others, true). Good nutrition is essential for health and should not become a bone (more likely a candy) of contention. Keeping promises (on both sides), doing what one says one is going to (both of you) and performing expected duties (home-work) and chores (dishes? dusting? lawn-mowing?) may be flexible but not negotiable. All members of the family have to contribute to the well-being and smooth-functioning of the organism, according to their abilities. Living by certain standards of behaviour, whether based on the religion of your choice or on society's laws and compassion's admonitions, may also be subject for discussion but not much leeway when it comes to basics (like theft or bodily harm). You'd be surprised how many children think those areas are negotiable, not to say malleable, and how many parents are manipulated into angry or helpless arguments or pleas to restore order. That's when the power struggle takes place, and it's no fun for either party.

Four No's

There are only four no's a parent should use with children:

- The life-saving no. You have to explain not only why you're saying no, but also the dangers involved in letting them run across a crowded street, or get into a stranger's car, or whatever.
- The challenge no. You can let them try something beyond their capacity, provided it won't kill them if they fail. Don't inhibit them; just warn them of the possibility of failure. "Go ahead," I heard a mother say to her kid who wanted to climb a tree. "You're insured."
- The character-building no. If they're not going to come home in time for dinner, or observe their curfews, then you have to be firmer about your no's, don't you? A good firm no can build character when it is consistent and fair. (I was inconsistent about my preferences and my impatience level. I guess I was the one who needed character-building.)
- The convenience no. Not to be used too often. There are times when a yes is beyond the physical, financial or other limits of the parents. Parents have rights, too.

Learn to Negotiate

If you have reached an impasse, as labour does when it is at loggerheads with management, then it is time to negotiate (see conflicts, page 103). Here is what you must do: Talk. Listen. Confer. Listen. Consult. Listen. Parley. Listen. Arrange terms. Listen. Suggest. Listen. Give a little. Take a little. Know the difference. Listen some more. "Sign" an agreement. Keep on listening.

These skills are as useful in a marriage counsellor's office as they are within a family.

Parents' Rules

Here are a few rules for the parents to keep in mind:

- Make clear the difference between a rule and a preference. There will be things you would rather your children didn't do, but you can't legislate everything. "Stop that noise" is usually a preference, unless someone in the house is ill or on a night-shift and sleeping days.

Don't change the rules arbitrarily according to your anger or inconvenience.Do change the rules upon negotiation and discussion, as the children grow older and more responsible.

Rules Is Rules

Some things, as I said, are not negotiable. You have to set clear, firm, consistent, age-appropriate family rules. (And as few rules as possible, please.) Some families impress and absorb these rules by osmosis, as it were. Others seem to find it necessary to write them down. Still others not only write them down but also accompany them with consequences if they're not adhered to. If you do that, then try not to paint yourself into a corner. Don't make the consequence impossible for either party to follow through on. You have to be as firm as your rule in order for it to be effective.

Every broken rule must have a consequence, else the rule has no effect. Even if it's inconvenient for the parent to follow through, it must be done. That's why it's a good idea not to have too many rules. The fewer the rules, the fewer to be broken and the fewer the consequences. Make sure the rules are important ones. As far as the actual consequences are concerned, grounding usually works best. No corporal punishment, no humiliation – both are tantamount to abuse. Tact doesn't hurt.

Three Things Children Need

1. Limits. Limits free children, give them a feeling of security, help them know how far they can push and what is the pale beyond which they must not venture. Spell it out for

them so they'll know. If they can't observe the limits, if they aren't ready to meet the restrictions or handle the freedom, then impose stricter limits. That is the clearest consequence of breaking the rules.

2. Autonomy. If greater freedom is granted as children go along, feel ready and ask for it, then it is accompanied by a feeling of pride for having earned it and of self-respect for being deemed worthy of it. Most parents make the mistake of underestimating their children's maturity and skills and of trying to keep them young and under wraps for too long, particularly the eldest child, whom you'll often hear yelling, "It isn't fair. I wasn't allowed to do that until I was ten!" When a younger sibling is granted whatever privilege it is at an earlier age, you can explain that you, too, have learned something, mostly from the good example the eldest child set you.

3. Attention. The reason a lot of kids stop telling their parents anything is that a lot of parents don't pay any attention to what their kids are saying. It's amazing how many parents don't listen to their kids. An absent "That's nice, dear" won't do when they're telling you something important. And when they have something to negotiate, then you must give them full attention and gravity. Listening should start very young, when what's being said isn't always terribly interesting. You can't edit a child; you listen and you accept. Then when you (and they) are older, you might be entitled to interpret and advise.

The Mad Fishwife

I can't stand this. I sound as if I know everything. Listen, do as I say, don't do as I did. I want you to know right now that I yelled at my kids. I was unfair, inconsistent, impatient and an adrenaline addict. When I got angry, my anger rose with my rising voice. Often an innocent misdemeanor could cause a court-martial as far as my tongue was concerned. Unfair, unfair. When I calmed down, I was overcome with remorse and guilt and asked my children's forgiveness. (Three of them forgave me.)

"Children," said Oscar Wilde, "begin by loving their parents; after a time they judge them; rarely, if ever, do they forgive them." That's why grandchildren were invented: to give you another chance. This time you can run a popularity contest, which some parents – especially the ones without custody – try to do.

To Yell or Not to Yell

I don't yell as much now, not because I have improved but because my children have. And there's no one to yell at.

I remember a character called Agnes in a novel by Angela Thirkell. Agnes had more children than I did, but she also had excellent help. When one of her children fell into a mud puddle, Agnes admonished the child mildly: "Wicked one! Wicked one! Go see Nanny."

I was struck dumb with admiration for such forbearance. But, you see, I didn't have a nanny. I was the nanny. If a kid of mine got muddy, I was the one who had to clean up the mess. So I said more than Agnes did, a lot more, quite loudly, and with some feeling. It seemed to give me energy as I cleaned up the mess.

It still comforts me to quote Pearl Buck: "Some are kissing mothers and some are scolding mothers, but it is love just the same, and most mothers kiss and scold together." Does that make you feel better, too?

Ten Ways to Turn Out Terrific Kids

Here's a neat list I came across in a recent *Reader's Digest*. It's by Ray Maloney, and it says it all (almost all, or I wouldn't be writing this guide).

1. Love them.
2. Build their self-esteem.
3. Challenge them.
4. Listen to them.
5. Expect respect.
6. Limit them.
7. Make God a part of their lives.
8. Develop a love of learning.

9. Help them be community-minded.

10. Let them go.

Maybe that's the kind of post-hypnotic suggestions they can get through life on.

What Do You Want for Your Children?

The question most parents want to ask about their children is *how*? How do you give your kids a sense of personhood, and how do you get the idea into them about being responsible for themselves and for other people, and what about morality, and will they be happy, and can we be friends?

All this eagerness and anxiety comes with an overload of guilt. "Dear God," prays every conscientious new mother, "help me to be a good mother," already worried that she won't be. I'm not sure what fathers pray. If songs and the popular culture are to be believed, they hope their sons will be able to play football with them (remember "My Boy Bill" from *Carousel*?) and that they'll grow up just like their pa. Very few women wish their daughters to grow up like them; they hope they'll be better.

What's "better"? Happier? More competent? More successful? Better adjusted (to what?)? I found out what I really wanted for my children when I had a damaged child. I wanted him to be an independent, functioning human being (and he is, with a lot of help from his community). That, basically, is what we all want for our children. Independent and functioning aren't too hard to define, but what do we mean by human being, and how do you create one?

Aha, you see, that's what families are for!

CHAPTER EIGHT

Children of Working Parents

Who takes the child by the hand, takes the mother by the heart.
— *Danish proverb*

Day Care

I've talked to enough working mothers to know how split they feel about leaving their children in day care. No matter how carefully they have chosen the facility, they still feel it could be better or they should be there, and they keep wondering if they've made the right choice. After they've agonized over the facilities, they go back to agonizing over the choice. Given all the other choices made before this one, they have no choice.

First Things First

In her no-nonsense little book called *The Working Parents' Guide to Child Care*, Bryna Siegel-Gorelick distinguishes between professional care-givers – nursery schools, child-care centres and so on – and in-home care-givers, be they members of the family, live-in or -out help (au pair girls, day-housekeepers, nannies, etc.). In every case, they should be paid (except, you'll have noticed, mothers). Even if you are destitute and dependent on the child-care services of a relative or neighbour, that person must be paid, if not in money then in some kind of reciprocal service. This is how parent co-ops were first formed, based on mutual help. Only by paying for services rendered can you be assured of what to expect and what to demand.

What to Consider in a Care-giver

Since child care is substitute mothering, it pays to do the choosing as carefully as you can. Take the time to interview carefully the prospective care-giver(s). Take some time to observe the operation of the child-care centre (some centres require it of the parents). Take time to adjust the child (and yourself) to the arrangement – and to the separation. Above all, take quality time with your child in the mornings and evenings when you are home. Here are some things to consider in a care-giver:

- age (and stamina)
- gender and attitudes (there are still a lot of male-chauvinist women out there)
- speech, language (this person will be a primary source of your child's first language lessons; it would be nice if it were grammatical)
- training/experience
- identity, meaning self-esteem, a satisfaction with the job, and the recognition that the work is worth doing
- TLC (if the person is incapable of this, she (or he?) shouldn't be in the job)

Practical Considerations

If you're taking your child out to day care, then consider location, size, cleanliness, equipment (including toys), supplies and, of course, cost. And give a thought to tax deductions, whatever subsidy is available, because no one else does, not yet, not consistently.

Consider the ratio of care-giver to child. For children from three to five years, the maximum should be fifteen to one (fewer is better). Under three, the ratio makes all the difference – between being cuddled and cared for and stimulated or being parked in a crib all day and left to fester in a dirty diaper.

Workplace Day Care

Little by little, private enterprise is getting into day care, recognizing it for the necessity it is. Here and there, unions are helping parents by pressuring management and gaining the support of governments at the local level to establish programs in the areas they are needed. One of the chief drawbacks of private day-care arrangements is often the distance from the home or workplace, thus involving extra time for delivery and pick-up of the child. Workplace day care can resolve this problem. There are, of course, some basic arrangements between both parties (the care-giving institution and the parent) before an on-site program can be launched.

What Do You Do When There's Sickness?

No matter what kind of care your child is in, there's going to be sickness, partly because of increased exposure to other children's germs. One of the biggest open secrets of nursery-level day care is the rampant exchange of gastroenteritis among babies. A family physician told me there are cases of babies in day care contracting giardiasis, which is contracted for life. Apart from that chilling prospect, the parents must have some alternate plans for days when the child is too sick to go out. This involves some decision-making at home.

Usually the parent earning the lowest income stays home with the sick child, because the economic risk in case of job loss is lower. Fathers also admit, however, that they suffer a certain loss of face if they are the ones on call. Care of the sick child is still considered women's work. Many employee interviews require women to reveal their child-care arrangements, while rarely questioning the men. It is still assumed that somewhere, somehow, a woman is taking care of all that. Employers also assume, as Letty Cottin Pogrebin comments, "that workers will rob their personal lives to pay for their economic survival rather than upset traditional male-female power relations." In other words, child care is still considered the responsibility of the mother.

Perhaps if employers realized that people would prefer not to destroy their personal lives or sacrifice their children for their jobs, attitudes about workplace day-care provision (and responsibility) would change. But most parents haven't yet come to that realization or to the willingness to dig their heels in and make their priorities clear, so how can they convince their employers? Every family considers its own case so individual and personal that every time they hit a crisis parents think they're making a unique choice, special to them and to this one occasion. They keep on juggling their own lives and the lives of their children without realizing that others are doing the same thing. Again, it's a matter of getting your priorities straight, and then of realizing you are not alone.

One of the arguments against workplace day care is that the employee becomes dependent on it and cannot leave his or her job for the sake of the child's continuity. How long does this bind last? School takes over from day care sooner or later, so the placement isn't forever. A small wave of young mothers is beginning to choose to stay at home for those tender day-care years, taking a short sabbatical from their work if they can afford to. Not many can, though – not the ones who need day care the most.

Why Can't They See?

It would behoove both the government and the private sector to help make day care available, feasible and affordable. The myth of the nuclear family persists longest in the minds of governments when it comes to child care. Economic factors being what they are, the double income family is here to stay. Governments are quick enough to tax the income a working wife may earn. They're going to have to realize that day care is a national necessity. Employers, also – those who want undivided loyalty from their employees – are going to have to help to provide safe, adequate, convenient, affordable workplace day care. They have to realize that while you can take the day care out of the mother you can't take the mothering out of day care.

Quality Time in the Rush Hour

Mornings are hardest. You put a run in your last decent pair of panty hose (or popped two buttons on a shirt? – I'm trying to be generic about this), find you have to press a skirt, cut yourself shaving, whatever. Hard enough to get adults ready to face Show Time! Harder for young children who make transitions less easily, no matter how much they like their day-care situation.

It helps to plan ahead. You can't quite foresee the run or the cut, but you could promise yourself never to run out of panty hose again, or try opening your eyes *before* you shave. In any case, have everything ready from the night before so you don't have to think in the morning. (It's very hard for most people to think in the morning.) Know what clothes you're going to wear and check that they're ready. Set the breakfast table, know what you're going to eat. Have everything everyone needs in neat piles at the door, ready to go: work, files, cleaning to go, show-and-tell to take. (Don't you wish, just once, you could walk out the door without carrying something?)

I know a lot of people who purposely get up an hour earlier than they have to. This hour is when they do their jogging or aerobics or just quietly read the paper. I know one man who gets up early to read the Bible. He's read it twice through, and he's not even that old. That inspired me, but I couldn't get past Leviticus. The point is that if you're all ready and relaxed you'll find it a lot easier to get your children ready without pressure.

Little kids hate to be pushed. They respond by baulking more, finding ways to dawdle and delay that can drive you up the wall, especially if you're pushed for time. You could avoid arguments by laying out a "scarecrow" of the children's clothes on the floor for them to get into – they like to do things for themselves at that certain age. But give them choices, too, so that they don't feel the need to assert themselves. "Would you like red or yellow socks?" (Sometimes they want both, one of each. So who's it going to kill?) "Shall I brush your hair before or after breakfast?" "Do you want peanut butter or honey on your toast?" (We all know the answer to that one, don't we?)

Don't spring things too fast on any child. Give him or her a few subtle warnings of what's to come, not only in the next twenty minutes but also tomorrow and next week. So: "As soon as I finish my coffee, we'll leave." "Tomorrow so-and-so is coming to look after you when I go to my meeting." "I must remember to get more cereal/peanut butter/bubble bath before we go away next weekend." This is basic communication, letting everyone in on what's happening. Later, your kids might even tell you such things.

Getting Along with the Routine

Some little kids are into ritual. Everything must be done just so, in exactly the same rigid order. This can be very time-consuming, especially in the morning when you have only three minutes to get out of the house. But you can use it to your advantage if you know the routine. (Know the routine! You could do it asleep, and you wish you were.) "Tuck your doll into bed before we put your jacket on." "You have one and a half minutes to walk backwards around the kitchen table – I don't suppose you could do it in one and a half minutes."

Children are also often reluctant to leave the activity at hand. Again, plan ahead, out loud. "You can finish colouring that picture when we get home." (That usually goes over like a lead balloon.) "Would you like me to colour a picture with you when we come back?" (That's better, but keep your promise.) The nice thing about this approach is that it reminds the child that you're coming back, that after the day apart, you will be together again, at home.

Young parents practise togetherness with their kids. When they're home now, they're really home. In my day, sitters were legion, and we would race out at night to meetings and movies, plays and parties, to make up for the days spent at home with the little ones. Now, young working parents usually spend their time after work with their children and seldom go out as a couple. They stay home reading to the kids, doing laundry and household chores, or they take the kids with them, shopping, to dinner, to parties, on trips. Talk about your quality time! It looks pretty quantitative, too. That's in the early years, of course. Later, when the children get older, running the family becomes more a question of traffic control than child care, and the fridge door becomes information headquarters.

You Deserve a Break Today

One area of the marketplace has responded to the needs of the busy family more quickly than others: the fast food outlets where eating out is a family entertainment, with clowns and games and toys, and where speed guarantees that even a very small child will eat something before boredom and restlessness set in. Hotels, too, have family rates, and resorts often have special "kids' villages" and separate programs to give the parents a chance to spend money on their own activities.

In the fifties, *McCall's* magazine started the togetherness theme: the family that plays together stays together, and all that (to us, now) rather maudlin sentiment that went hand in oven mitt with somethin' lovin' cookin' in the oven. As one of the parents responsible for that Big Boom generation, I can tell you we practised a lot of togetherness. But in many ways it wasn't as genuine as the togetherness of today's families, and this, surprisingly, in a decade when even very young kids are sent out to be cared for and picked up at the end of each day in accordance with their parents' working hours.

What About a Nanny or Housekeeper?

A lot of mothers are not comfortable with the thought of group day care – not only mixing all those germs but losing one-on-one attention. They want something more exclusive than that, in or out of the home. I know one young couple who found a young woman who was trained as a nanny to whom they could deliver their child and, soon, their two very young children (only fourteen months apart). The fact that the nanny lived across the street from their house was sheer luck. This nanny had two preschool children of her own, and that was all she took on. She gave her young charges daily exercise and fresh air, nutritious hot lunches, consistent discipline, stimulating activity and her undivided attention. She also gave her employers the benefit of flex-time. It sounded too good to last, and it was. Nanny's husband moved out of the city, and she went with him.

Other families prefer a live-in or at least an in-home nanny; some of them come in by the day but prefer not to be resident. There are now, as you might expect, a couple of books on the choosing and keeping of nannies (see Bibliography, page 210), including a discussion of the different types available, techniques of interviewing, a discussion of salary and other ways of keeping a jewel when you've found one. I imagine they have a few tips for nannies, too.

What everyone thinks they want, of course, is a Mary Poppins, but she was a very versatile nanny, and you might pause and decide what aspects you liked best. Some mothers want security and routine for their children; others want good English and decent manners; others are sticklers for cleanliness, regular fresh air and good nutrition. Bear in mind you can't have everything and bear in mind what your priorities are as you begin interviewing. Also bear in mind that you are looking for an employee not a bosom buddy. A certain amount of loyalty can be bought; friendship is an unsolicited gift and one that you have no right to expect. You can earn loyalty and respect by being a fair employer and by not trying to chisel more service or time out of your nanny/housekeeper than you contracted for.

Older Children

What about school-age children? School reduces the cost of

day care but it presents other problems, not the least of them being, what do you do in the summer? You take a look at the Y and community day camp programs, sign the kids up for sailing or pottery courses, or, if you can afford it, send them off to a boarding camp for at least part of the summer. It costs.

As for school, again the big question is, what happens when the child is sick, and also when there is a Professional Development Day, or whatever a school day off is called in your area? It's not a teachers' day off – the teachers are usually working – but it takes place during school time and it puts pressure on parents because the kids are at loose ends. Choices have to be made about them: who's going to fill in the gap? As always, alternate arrangements are essential in case of emergency.

Latchkey Children

School hours don't match work hours. Usually the parents have to be at work before the child has to be at school and don't return until after school has let out. And so we have what are known as latchkey children, kids who let themselves into the house and who take care of themselves until the parent or parents get home (a lot of them are single-parent homes). After I was widowed, my youngest child became a latchkey child for a time. I signed him up for after-school courses, programs run by volunteers (parents themselves) from the Home and School Association. The kids learned cooking, dramatics, macramé, floor hockey and so on, yet the real purpose of this extra-curricular education was to keep the kids occupied and off the streets until their parents got home from work. At the inner-city school Matt attended, children of single and one-income parents were given priority.

I have spoken to teachers at schools across the country where, not by legislation but out of kindness and concern, a teacher will come early each day and open the school so that there is a place for children whose parent(s) must leave home before they do. I also know teachers who keep a box of cereal in their desk drawer for kids who haven't had breakfast, and I knew one principal who had a couple of extra cots put into the First Aid room so that children who needed sleep more than education might get some rest. Unsung social workers, all.

And then we have Block Parents, a continent-wide phenomenon whose major catalyst was probably the anxiety of working mothers. Block Parents, as everyone must know by now, are people at home who display a sign in their window to indicate their willingness to help a child in distress. The "Block Parent" sign tells a child that someone trustworthy is available in case of an emergency.

Knowing where help is available and how to get it is a necessary skill even for very young children these days. I know single mothers who teach their children their names and phone numbers and how to dial the emergency number before they teach them nursery rhymes. It's a survival skill, just as watching out for sabre-toothed tigers must have been in eons past. You can go further with older children and put them through fire drills or emergency behaviour. "What would you do if . . ." and test them for their knowledge of exits, location and use of the fire extinguisher (if they're old enough to handle it), and, of course, the phone numbers.

Here's a list of rules from a working mother for her latchkey children:

- no cooking (microwave excepted),
- no friends, no visitors,
- keep the doors locked,
- don't open the door to strangers,
- don't admit you're alone and don't give away parents' absence on the phone either (better yet, don't answer – I used to have a signal for my kids when I wanted them to answer; you could work this out in advance),
- don't go out (or, for older kids, leave a note if you do, stating where you have gone, with a phone number).

The Working Child

The working child (that is, the child of working parents) develops some other skills before long. As the kid gets older and more competent (not necessarily more responsible), Mother starts phoning about four-thirty every afternoon to issue instructions about dinner. "You'll find a casserole on the third shelf of the fridge. Take it out and turn the oven on to 350°F. When the light goes out, put the casserole in the oven. You might tear up some lettuce for a salad, if you feel like it."

Working single mothers save all their housework until Sunday afternoon. They throw the laundry in (if you time it right in an apartment building, you can do four or five wash loads at once), one of the kids vacuums, another dusts, the little one (that many kids?) empties the wastebaskets. When both parents work, the chores become a family affair, particularly for the single parent family. Children can be remarkably helpful. Before you start getting maudlin and too grateful, remember that they still don't hang up their wet towels or put their clothes anywhere but on the floor.

Kids do, however, develop some sense of responsibility and become quite competent at domestic duties, more so than chldren of stay-at-home mothers. I know a fifteen-year-old boy who makes a mean BLT and who even offers to make it for other family members since he has the knife out. I suppose it would be too much to ask him to clean up the kitchen?

Other Working Children

There are other working children – kids who have part-time jobs. I am tempted to say that such employment is more common among children of single parents, but I know this is not necessarily so. Some families manage to get along only by dint of every able-bodied person in the household working.

I know more young people than I can count who regularly hold down part-time jobs and juggle their school work as well as extra-curricular activities with scarcely a break in their rhythm. I have nothing but admiration for them. A working student, though, is still a child and needs help to keep in balance. There is still the major commitment to his or her education that must be honoured. A job must not be permitted to interfere too drastically with study time, sleeping time and other necessities. At the same time, the responsibility to the employer must be met.

One boy who had a part-time job at a discount store had to skip a couple of school days for stock-taking. He was reluctant to do this because he had a perfect attendance record. However, he discussed the problem with his parents and with his employer and agreed to give the time required to his job. That's what I mean by balance.

I know a young girl who gave her employers a dressing down for keeping her up too late baby-sitting on a school night. She needed her sleep, she said, and wouldn't be able to help them on weeknights if they didn't honour their part of the contract.

Both those young people, I think, had good parents. What you can do, as parents of working children, is support them in their work, make sure they still get proper meals, especially when their hours are erratic, and be grateful you have such responsible kids.

CHAPTER NINE

Siblings/The Only Child

My brother was an only child. — *Jack Douglas*

"Mom always liked you best." You've heard that line so often it has become almost every family's family joke (if the family has siblings); comedian Tom Smothers parlayed it and a pout into fame and fortune.

Sibling Rivalry Even people who never cracked a psychology book know the term *sibling* and the phrase *sibling rivalry*. Magazine and armchair psychologists never run out of wise things to say about the achieving older sibling, the quiet middle one, the scrappy youngest. It's watered-down Adler (one of Freud's early brights), and we still live by his stereotypes. We know all about the Hard Knocks Eldest, the Neglected Middle Child, the Me-Too Baby, the Prodigal Son, the Scapegoat, the Sneaky One, the Tattle-Tale and so on. Only recently have we been warned to beware of type-casting, of self-fulfilling prophesies (don't tell your kid he's lazy if you don't want him to be). We all send messages, especially subliminal ones, especially in families.

Busy parents are urged to be impartial, to give one-on-one attention to each child, to encourage the younger one without holding back the older ones, to arbitrate the fights and teach civil rights as well as table manners. But parents are human, too, and they're still siblings themselves, still struggling with their own private demons of jealousy and impossible impositions and the surrogate roles (Little Mother, Good Child, Big Spender) they were saddled with.

Where, but in the bosom of one's family, can one learn moral outrage, the rankling sense of injustice when one's siblings are treated better than oneself? Where else can one learn so early and so well that life isn't fair, nor was ever meant to be? Who else but a sibling can teach you to play harder, run faster, and think smarter if you want to get ahead – and if that doesn't work, how to slow others down to your pace? Siblings teach each other language: "The word is not *keputz*," a know-it-all older sister was heard insisting loudly to her younger brother at a fast-food restaurant, "it's kep-shit!" And she dumped some on his French fries.

Special Cases

Sometimes, as in my family, there is a special case. My youngest son is brain-damaged. (I tell our story in *The Book of Matthew*.) I remember once I came home from a gruelling diagnostic test Matt had undergone (and failed) at the hospital to be greeted by his sister Liz with the news that she had won an art contest. It was good news but fraught with danger! Half the trick is not to lean too hard on other children's successes as compensation so that they feel they have to perform and produce to make up for the damaged one. And half the trick is not to downplay their success (to avoid hurting the feelings of the one who can never hope to live up to their standards) and so deny the achiever her due share of praise.

What I learned was not to be a comparison shopper, to accept each child's achievements for what they were and to expect the best that each child was capable of. Matt's siblings had to learn compassion, patience and tolerance. Oh, and forgiveness. (His brother never quite learned that; subconsciously he still feels that Matt cheated him of too much.)

Other Lessons

So you learn diffidence and resentment in a family. You can also learn charm and humour. Haven't you noticed how members of the same family laugh alike, or sound like each other on the phone? Families often have the same group sense of humour. As long as it's not at the expense of one particular member all the time, it can be fascinating and delightful.

I was only five years old when my grandfather died, but I sat at his dinner table most of my formative life. He was a demanding host: he wanted to be entertained at table. Everyone in his family (my father and my aunts and uncles) learned at an early age to tell a good story with a good punch line. Those who weren't telling it were rooting for it, with encouragement and laughter. That same style carried over into family gatherings long after my grandfather was gone. I sometimes think one of the subliminal reasons I married my husband was that my grandfather would have enjoyed him. Bill was a good dinner partner. Laughter is good relish for a meal, whether it's company or family.

Group Lessons

I have known siblings with secret codes, passwords and elaborate plans to defeat the enemy. I've seen siblings in a family (including mine) band together in times of adversity and rally round with a fortitude and wisdom it would be impossible to teach or buy. Human siblings are almost like the Midwich cuckoos in John Wyndham's novel, so uncanny are they in their organic communication and self-protection.

But they are also disparate. "Make her stop teasing me!" is still a cry from younger siblings wherever they are. There was always a sister to teach her brother how to dance, or a brother to teach his sister how to throw straight. (Stereotypes!)

Siblings also learn the meaning of unconditional acceptance for the sole fact that they are family. In a nurturing family they learn to be themselves, but they also learn the satisfaction of being responsible for others, of being trusted to carry out their responsibilities. They learn self-esteem not only from their parents' expectations and praise but also from their siblings' appreciation of them. They learn solidarity.

The Brotherhood of Man?

Much as I hate the sexist language of the above phrase, it is an example of an idea that may fade from usage, along with, for example, fraternity, sisterhood, blood brother, all because the reality it is based on no longer exists. (Maybe even nepotism will die!) Family connections and loyalties will lose their strength because there will be so few people to whom one owes that kind of devotion. The blood that used to be thicker than water will run thinner and thinner from generation to generation, if, in fact, it regenerates at all.

The family is the crucible where siblings learn their first lessons about the unfairness of life, the skills of negotiation, the value of an ally, and the importance of group loyalty. What happens in a family where no such lessons are learned because there's only one child? Where does the child learn how to fight, to make up, to share, to survive, to love, and to be responsible for others if there are no others? Maybe life is easier if no favourites are played, but is it real? Rumours are sifting in from China that one-child families are changing an entire nation's attitude to communism. If there's only one child, who has to learn how to share? That's not the only concept that may go begging in a world of single-child families.

Robert Glossop asks these questions: What happens to all the metaphors – brotherliness, sisterliness, he/she has been like a brother/sister to me? What happens to societies and companies: fraternal societies, fraternal orders – upon which many unions are based – family companies, companies that are run like families? What happens to a society that doesn't have these qualities built in? In short, what happens to the brotherhood of man if every family has, at most, one only, lonely child? Glossop doesn't know the answers, nor do we, because the returns aren't in yet.

Society as a whole has always tended to move back and forth between the close, tight, protective support of the family unit and the looser, wide-ranging network of the community, often balancing one against the other. If the family unit becomes too small, there is only community. Will it provide the necessary support? Can it stand the strain? Without kin, we're all going to have to learn how to be kind. Can we?

The Only Child

Poor lonely only child, so the myth goes, with no one to play with, pampered and indulged, even spoiled, but neglected by the adults who are too intent on their own lives to pay attention to the child. Not so, say only children; it's not like that at all. For one thing, I am told, they don't get spoiled. Since an only child is the only one to do the family proud, expectations of performance are higher than normal. In the event of failure, blame is focussed rather harshly, and there is no one to share it. Certainly the incidence of achievers among only and eldest children is very high.

An only child told me she was never neglected or ignored by her parents. Far from it, in fact. They included her in their activities from an early age. I see it now among the young families I know. Only children get taken everywhere – it's cheaper than leaving them at home with a sitter. They quickly learn to behave well and develop a poise far beyond their years. As Benjamin Spock said: "Perhaps a child who is fussed over gets a feeling of destiny, he thinks he is in the world for something important and it gives him drive and confidence."

As for the give-and-take of sibling rivalry, I am told that only children get that in day care now. Surveys indicate that day-care children demonstrate a far greater degree of sociability, co-operation (and also aggressiveness) than stay-at-home children. It doesn't matter whether they are only children or siblings, they develop different responses when exposed to the give-and-take of day care.

Day care is not the only group activity that provides the only child with the experience of getting along with other children. There are, as they get older, organized sports and other activities, all involving group co-operation, as well as summer camps, both boarding and day. In fact, these days, very few young people are alone for long at whatever age. They seem to be processed in herds and to move in packs and to find their stability and self-image among their peers.

Statistics

I hope this is comforting to parents today who are having fewer children than their parents and even fewer than their grandparents. Canada's birth rate is about 1.7 children per family now, lower than simple replacement requires. Families are having one, at most two, children, and some of them worry that they are depriving their children of the camaraderie of their own families.

I am a firm believer in compensation. As the saying goes, when a door closes, a window opens. I see today's young families sharing child care, excursions and special events with their siblings and their children. In other words, cousins enjoy a larger family life. The advantage to this is that cousins can be same age and same sex, something that is possible within a nuclear family only in the case of twins. The other advantage is that cousins go away, back to their own homes, so that little girls don't have to put up with whiny little brothers or bullying big ones, and little boys don't have to be nice to their little sisters or stop hitting their know-it-all big ones. It's easier to ignore a cousin. So they get the pleasure of almost-siblings without the in-fighting.

If there aren't any cousins to bring together, young families will import a playmate for an only child: a friend is taken to the zoo or a picnic or a fair so the child has a companion to share the festivities with; a young guest can be invited for a week at a cottage with the family, or to go some place special for a long weekend. Lots of combinations are possible and are practised. Lonely only children aren't the only ones who don't have built-in companions.

Other Kinds, Other Problems

There are other kinds of only children. They used to be

known as afterthoughts – surprise babies born late to mature parents who thought they were past that sort of thing. These occur now more frequently to an older father who has remarried a younger woman who wants a child of her own. There is also the only child born to slightly younger parents who each perhaps has children from a former marriage but who together want a child of this union. In these cases, isolation by age may make the child seem only, though he or she may have half-brothers or -sisters, or steps, or even aunts or uncles of a similar age. (The combinations these days are mind-boggling.)

I talked to a number of parents of such "only" children of blended families. Many of them have confessed to me what seemed to them a fault they couldn't correct: they loved their own child, this fruit of the new union, more than they cared for the others, particularly the others from the spouse's previous marriage. It's understandable, blood and genes being what they are. But here is a new danger, a new source of rivalry and jealousy for the new generation of Smothers Brothers. The circumstances may be different, but the emotion is the same. How do you deal with it?

As one mother put it, "I may feel like hitting the others, but I clout my own." That's favouritism?

CHAPTER TEN

How to Understand a Teenager

To bring up a child in the way he should go,
Travel that way yourself once in a while.
— *Josh Billings*

A Stranger in Your Midst

Kids aren't the only ones who think they're changelings or that they've been dropped from outer space into an alien group. Parents think so, too, when a child reaches adolescence. Suddenly there is a stranger in your midst, someone who resists everything that is going on, denies the resistance, and doesn't want to talk about it anyway. After all you've done, you deserve better than this. This isn't what you had in mind at all. Or maybe – have you thought of this? – after all you've done, this is exactly what was programmed to happen. (Remember Harry Chapin's song "Cat's Cradle"?)

Parents' Self-Esteem

When our son John was about four, my husband and I spent an evening with a couple who had an eleven-year-old heller.

On the way home Bill congratulated himself that his son wasn't like that. I warned him not to be rashly optimistic. The next morning when church was over, Bill made the mistake of asking John's Sunday school teacher how the kid was doing.

"Just fine" was the sweet but harried reply, "but I do wish you'd ask him not to walk on the piano."

I knew a doctor who specialized in child care. What he didn't know about kids you could put in an eye dropper. So when his first child started school, he couldn't wait to be told what a good job he was doing on Super-Kid. He went with his wife to his first parent-teacher meeting.

"Well," said the kindergarten teacher looking him over with a beady, appraising eye, "you've certainly raised an aggressive child, haven't you?"

It's times like that that keep parents humble. Pride goeth, and all that. No matter how detached and mature you try to be, when it comes to your children, your self-esteem is tightly linked to their behaviour. It's unfair, as far as the kids are concerned, but there it is. You often forbid them to do something or get angry at them for something, not because of what it's doing to them but because of what it's doing to you, your pride, your expectations. What *did* you expect?

What Parents Want for Their Children

Merton P. Strommen and A. Irene Strommen define and prescribe for the "five cries of parents" in a book of the same name. They say these five "cries" are the parents' needs for their adolescent children:

• Understanding
• A close family
• Moral behaviour
• Shared faith
• Outside help

Understanding

Adolescence may be the time when the parents want the answers, but that's not when the problems started. Truth to tell, they probably started before the child was even born. Have you ever heard yourself talking (yelling?) at your kids and realized that you sounded exactly like your own parents? It's as if a tape recorder were running in your head and out come those words you hated to hear when you were young. From Michele Slung's book *More Momilies*, here are some of those echoes going round in your head.

- Don't get smart with me.
- That's not a face I'd advise you to make too often, young man/young lady.
- I'm not talking to you for my health.
- Look at me when I'm talking to you.
- If you fall out of that tree and break your leg, don't come running to me.
- If I wanted to know your opinion, I'd ask for it.
- You'd lose your head if it weren't tied on.
- Why can't you be more like your brother/sister?
- Don't talk with your mouth full.
- Share your toys.
- Good enough isn't good enough.
- You'll understand when you're older.
- If you don't stop crying, I'll give you something to cry about.
- I intend to spank you within an inch of your life.
- That's just a taste of what you'll get next time.
- Wait till your father gets home.

And here you are, an adult and a parent yourself, saying the same words, repeating patterns, spouting lines you never wanted to hear again. It takes a lot of conscious effort, even after the recognition, to get rid of them.

Add to whatever was in your memory banks new circumstances – death, divorce, financial problems, overwork, rejection, fear – and your terrible gut reactions to them, and there are times when you think you haven't grown up at all. You are not acting like an adult human being; in fact, you are not even acting – you are re-acting. Knee-jerk. Whoever said you had any business being a parent?

Where Did It All Begin?

Infancy is easy: you just have to keep the babies fed, clean and healthy, also stimulated, cuddled and reassured. It's when the child reaches adolescence that your problems begin. You can't solve their problems then with a Band-Aid and a kiss. And you can't tell them anything.

Did you ever think that maybe you don't have to try, that, in fact, you shouldn't, that maybe you should do more listening than telling? Your life is very different now from your parents' lives, you've probably commented on that yourself. Stop to think how different your children's lives are from yours. The old solutions simply don't apply, because the problems are not anywhere near the same. When you were twelve, you weren't being asked to make curriculum choices that could affect the rest of your life. When you were fourteen, no one was handing you advice on safe sex. Here's another joke. Two little kids on tricycles are having a chat.

"I found a package of condoms under the verandah," says one.

"What's a verandah?" asks the other.

The ad keeps flashing on the TV screen: "Do you know where your children are?" It could also say, "Do you know where your children are at?" I mean, do you really know what your children are worrying about? If you don't know, how can you help them or reassure them? Here's a list, from a survey taken among fifth-graders (that's pre-teen, just going into the crunchy time):

My Worries

- School performance
- My "looks"
- That a parent might die
- Hunger and poverty
- Violence in our country

- Losing a best friend
- Drinking by friends (or using drugs)
- Getting a job
- Physical development

Do any of them sound familiar?

Other Concerns

As they grow older, adolescents refine that list and add some other worries:

- Alcohol and drugs
- Sex
- Money
- Education
- One's personal future

Inside Stories

I have been privileged recently to read what some teenagers are thinking these days. Granted, these are the more articulate ones, with perhaps a little more insight into themselves given by the very act of writing. Nevertheless, they give me insight, too. Many of these young people are into fantasy, total escape from the pressures of here and now, some sci-fi, some magic. A number of them write pieces for children, creating whole wonderworlds with Seuss-like creatures and no rules – again, escape. But some of the older ones write about fear and pain and loss. Fear is surreal, threatening and incomprehensible, ominous feathers falling from a cloud, enveloping the mind in pressures that can't be fought.

Their pain is always emotional pain. At this age, young people think they're immortal and tend to ignore any temporary physical upset. The young person may be immortal, but significant adults are not. I have read stories in which an adolescent tries to come to terms with the death of a loved one, sometimes a parent, more often a grandparent. There are other kinds of loss to deal with, frequently the loss of a parent through separation or divorce. This loss is always accompanied by disillusion and an erosion of faith in people's promises and their ability (or intention) to keep them.

Add to these searing personal experiences, pressures of school and the peer group, the overwhelming onslaught of the hormones, and the need to define oneself as a person, unique and separate and not simply one interchangeable unit of the family cell, beginning usually with an invidious comparison with the other family members who are found wanting, especially the mother and father – and you have just met some of the main reasons why this creature in your midst is sullen, silent, unco-operative, uncommunicative, moody, intransigent and not much fun to be with. What ever happened to that cute little tyke who thought you were perfect?

It just happens that your kids are under terrific pressure, as much as or more than you are, and without the years of experience you've had in coping with it. It's no wonder a lot of them get a little tetchy. Look at what you do when you're spread too thin. It's stress, again, and has to be dealt with as such. (See stress, page 94.) Granted, it's harder for you to deal with when you meet with such resistance.

Suddenly you're the enemy: nothing you say is right, everything you do is suspect. Try not to take it too personally. In most cases, there's nothing wrong with your fifteen- to eighteen-year-old that being twenty-one won't cure. Try to keep your cool and also your warmth. Remember that you love this kid, this changeling, even if it is from another galaxy. Don't stop telling your children – even big and ungainly as they have become – that you love them. Never underestimate the power of repetition (look what it did for their teeth, reminding them to brush after meals!).

Role-Playing

I'll talk about the usefulness of games later (see page 112). Role-playing is another kind of game you might find illuminating. It can give both you and your teenager some insights into each other. Someone told me about playing it at a mother-daughter meeting she attended. This adult woman was assigned the role of a young girl who overhears her mother telling a friend on the phone that her daughter has started to menstruate. My friend had to accost her "mother" and accuse her of telling her secrets, making light of what was very important to her. Suddenly she was thirteen again, tearful, emotional, shrill, feeling betrayed and vulnerable and hating her "mother." She said it was a revelation.

It's also a revelation that may be hard to bear if you get your teenagers to role-play you and their other parent. Make up a few situations for them to get their teeth into (examples from real life abound) and brace yourself. You'll find out who's really boss, who's unfair, who can be counted on in an emergency (if you didn't know it already). Kids are surprisingly accurate in their perceptions of their parents – surprisingly because you think they don't pay attention to a word you say.

If you think you can't stand it, start with Charades. About ten years ago.

As Ye Sow

Sometimes a high price has to be paid for the freedom parents enjoyed when their children were little. A great deal has been (or should have been) established long before the child becomes an adolescent. If children have been pawned off all their lives with junk food, junk comics, junk TV, junk schools and junk examples, advice and guidance from their parents, then there's going to be trouble when they have to make their own choices. Children need proper nourishment, for their bodies, their minds and their spirits. Families have it within their power to give children that nourishment, thus counter-acting the pressure of the peer group by the time adolescents begin to make their own decisions. They have a lot of decisions to make these days.

A teacher told me that she recently helped supervise a school dance for thirteen- and fourteen-year-olds. She was warned not to turn on the strobe lights for dramatic effect, not for the sake of any epileptics who might be in the crowd but for the sake of those who were drunk. Apparently if you've been drinking you fall down when a strobe light mixes up your boozy brain waves. Someone turned on the strobe, though, and half the kids fell down. Do they really enjoy it?

Peer pressure suggests that it's cool to participate in whatever activity is popular. Rebelliousness incites an adolescent to go against the family standards. (Question: Does the family have standards?) Uncertainty causes bravado, trying to make it look like conviction. So teenagers test rules, bend or break curfews and flaunt outrageous behaviour.

A Close Family Life

Be assured. Experts tell us that close family life, impossible as it may seem to you if you are living in the eye of the storm, is one of the major strengths that adolescents have. If you can give them that strength, you – and they – are ahead. What is actually going on in a healthy (noisy) family all the time, subliminally or whatever, is a continuous dialogue. Note: to an outsider it may sound like fighting; to family members it is an intense internal communication. If close family life is the strength of the teenager, then the dinner table is the strength of family life. (See dinner, page 125.) If family members learn their lines well enough, they'll be able to handle the United Nations when they get to that level. (The U.N. was never like this, because their dinner table isn't big enough to accommodate everyone.)

Like the U.N., a family needs some basic, humanitarian laws to live by. These are also called values, or even morals (See morals, page 138). It needs flexibility, especially in the parents, and a willingness to negotiate (See negotiating, page 103), coupled with common sense and good judgement. It needs to be both fair and consistent, but also swift in its fair, consistent action. This is known as discipline (see rules, page 55). Ruptures and conflicts must be handled in a forthright, positive way. As with the U.N., at no time, ever, may communications be allowed to break off (see communication, page 111). No matter what you do, keep talking. As Winston Churchill said about the United Nations, "Jaw, jaw, jaw, is better than war, war, war" (you have to pronounce it right).

A sense of humour helps. As one little kid put it, "I like my family because they make me laugh."

Sometimes, though, it's no laughing matter.

Adolescent Suicide

Eyes, look your last!
Arms, take your last embrace! and lips, O you
The doors of breath, seal with a righteous kiss
A dateless bargain to engrossing death!
— Thus with a kiss I die.
> — Shakespeare, *Romeo and Juliet*

A Death in the Family

When I was almost grown-up, I knew one young person, a few years younger than I was then, who tried to commit suicide and succeeded on his second attempt. He shot himself. (Is that one of the reasons I would never have a gun in my home?) Among people I know, one woman has lost *two* sons to suicide. She's sober now. I can't think of anyone else. It's not something people talk about easily.

You hear of high school kids who go berserk with a gun, hold the school at bay, shoot their buddies and themselves. The story makes arresting headlines, and you wonder why. Less dramatic are the kids who O.D., or do something stupid and fatal while stoned: my kids knew a teenaged boy who drove his snowmobile into a barbed wire fence and was decapitated. Is that suicide? Almost, though not quite planned.

Some Statistics

Over the past decade or so in North America there has been a 30 to 35 percent increase in adolescent (ages ten to twenty-four) suicide. The figure varies according to what country, province or state the kids live (die) in. Suicide is the second-highest killer of people this age. As you might expect, accidents rank highest. For every successful (?) suicide, there are ten attempts. Many of those who try and fail to kill themselves the first time are not merely grandstanding to get sympathy or attention; they'll succeed the next time. Why? Why do they do it?

Causes of Adolescent Suicide

• Depression

- Loss of parent through death, divorce, separation or even long absence
- Alienation from family
- Breakdown of communication
- A change of address away from one's friends, and perhaps a special friend
- Break-up with a friend, usually but not necessarily of the opposite sex
- Fear of world events
- The mystic attraction of death

Warning Signs of a Possible Suicide
Verbal signs
- "I wish I were dead"
- "No one needs me"

Behavioural signs
- mood shifts
- an attempt

Depression
- fatigue
- loss of appetite/energy
- withdrawal from friends
- spending time alone
- difficulty sleeping
- talk about suicide
- giving away prized possessions
- helplessness
- feelings of guilt
- low self-esteem
- delinquent behaviour
- sexual promiscuity
- drug and alcohol abuse
- drop in grades and/or quality of schoolwork

Does it sound like someone you know? The sad thing is that many of these behaviour patterns are those of a normal, mixed-up teenager. (Who would ever want to go back to those years?) The other sad thing is that the family, which is supposed to be the source of well-being, the recharging unit,

the support centre, is frequently the cause or at least the final
irritant that makes a young life appear unbearable. What can a
parent do? Where can parents turn?

You Are Not Alone
If you need outside help, look around and find it:
Professional:
- minister
- rabbi
- school counsellor, teacher
- family doctor
- psychiatrist

Community aid:
- church groups
- Y workshops
- community college courses
- Family Services (or whatever it's called in your area)

Groups:
- Al-Anon – if that's the family problem
- Bereaved Families Association (or whatever the name of it
  is where you are)
- networks – you name the problem, there's an association to
  help you deal with it

– **Books, tapes, information, expert resources**
– **Neighbours, friends, relatives**
– **Activity, perhaps generated by a support group. (Fun
  isn't bad, but what's even better is.)**
– **Service – getting involved in helping others**

One of the best ways to feel better, I have always found, is to
look around and find someone who needs help even more
than you do. It may help your child and you to get
involved – together – in a community project.

Anything Else?
I want to add: chicken soup, hugs and prayer. I'm not being
facetious. Chicken soup represents TLC, home comfort, the
concern and affection of people who are important to the
sufferer. It's well known that when we're sick or tired or

discouraged, we turn to comfort food, also known as nursery food. Ask anyone what they like to eat when they're recovering from flu or a love affair and they'll tell you what Mother used to bring on a tray. Chicken soup (with lots of noodles) is high on the list.

As for hugs, surely everyone knows by now how important hugs are. Leo Busacaglia makes a career of passing out hugs, verbal and physical. American psychologist Virginia Satir says we all need four hugs a day for survival, eight for maintenance and twelve for growth. She knows that hugs are not sexual; hugs are therapeutic. Families are one of the safest groups to get and give hugs in. They should be lavishly exchanged. "When I give you a hug, give me two hugs back," says Michael Reinberger (first Grade, Antioch, California). The trick is not to stop giving them just because the kid is bigger than you are. The life you save might be his.

Never Underestimate the Power

As for prayer, it doesn't matter what denomination or language the prayer is in, it is, as they say, the thought that counts. The important thing is the attempt to formulate one's thoughts and communicate them – to God within, God without. If the family, and the troubled child of the family, is fortunate enough to have a positive belief system, it's that much easier. It doesn't matter what you call Him/Her/It. Getting in touch with one's innermost feelings, gaining some insight into one's self, actually attempting to communicate some idea of one's problems, in private – that's what prayer is. Like chicken soup, it doesn't hurt and it might help.

God bless you!

CHAPTER ELEVEN

How to Handle Stress

The trouble with life in the fast lane is that you get to the other end in an awful hurry. — *John Jensen*

Stress: 1. constraining force; physical, mental, or emotional pressure or strain: stresses of urban living. 2. a state or condition resulting from such pressure or strain: suffering from stress. (*Gage Canadian Dictionary*)

I'm not for a minute suggesting that women stop running in the fast lane and go back to the kitchen. Staying home is a positive choice, not a negative solution. Stress is not a male prerogative, as women in the working world are now proving (women's smoking has increased, more than men's, and so have cigarette- and stress-related diseases among women).

Anyway, in my day women at home weren't stressed. Their doctors told them so. They were "restless"; they were dissatisfied; they didn't know a good thing when they had it, so they were told. They weren't properly grateful. They were prescribed Valium so they would be grateful. Stress, I mean real STRESS, belonged to the world of business. Not any more. Now with women working full-time and running the house in the forty or fifty hours of spare time they give to that, they're entitled to some stress of their own. And they're getting it.

Life in the Fast Lane

The career wife has her pressures. Do I have to tell you about it? She is learning that she must seek help for the stress she feels, trying to be all things to all people. Like most upper-middle-class achievers, she is addicted to perfection. Women's magazines are beginning to recognize her plight with humour, referring to her esoteric dinner parties (breast of squid on a mango leaf, with a sauce made of sun-dried raspberries, and for dessert a white chocolate reproduction of Picasso's *Guernica*); her achieving child (creating his own computer programs at age three); her prowess in her field (brain surgery on Siamese twins joined at the head, or mistress-minding a billion-dollar merger between two yogurt giants); her easy good looks, skin, hair, clothes; her divinely handsome husband who wouldn't dream of looking at another woman (but who, when he does, falls for the airhead who pampers him with meatloaf and oatmeal cookies).

Pick up any woman's magazine and you'll learn all you want to know about the latest balancing act women are performing, as well as tips on how to do it, make it look easy and stop feeling guilty. Men's mags are still into the perfect martini, hi-tech equipment and Calvin Klein look-alike contests. This is not to say that men are not under stress. They are.

Dr. Sam Luker, a family therapist and head of Family Studies at the University of Guelph, says that the new working woman is "terrifically impactful on men's self-esteem. Women," says Luker, "are finally reaching a status of equality, but they're going to have to pay the price." (Is that a threat?) The price is stress.

Doing It All

Doing it all has been the main theme of those magazine articles. There's a saying that describes the perfect woman as an angel in the parlour, a wizard in the kitchen, and a courtesan in the bedroom. Women have been trying to live up to that for centuries, adding a mamele in the nursery and a genius in the boardroom to their roles. They work full-time, rush home to do the shopping, the cooking, the cleaning, give quality time to the kids and keep the marriage "alive." No wonder they're almost dead. It's called role strain. Actually, it's called tired.

Are you sure it's stress? It might be plain old burnout.

The New Man

The New Man has changed his role, too. He isn't afraid to cry now, according to the (women's) magazines. He has entered the labour room with enthusiasm and can give a good back rub, carry a child (on his back or shoulders), cook up a mean stir-fry and help with the shopping. The key word is *help*. He still expects his wife to make the plans and the shopping list, and he'll help. Note that while men's attitudes have changed a lot – the majority surveyed now say they think husbands of working wives should help with the housework – their behaviour hasn't caught up with their belief. Most of them still don't help much.

A new survey has discovered that women who work full-time spend an average of sixty-four minutes a day on child care, while their husbands spend twenty-two minutes. As for the housework, when their wives go out to work full-time, men take on an extra nine minutes a day.

So women are not only anxious, guilty and tired; they're also not having much fun. We're supposed to have fun. Our hedonistic society requires it of us. More guilt. Now we have to program fun-time. Oh, joy.

Need Any More?

There's another cause of stress in both men and women, and that is women working. It's not the fact of the work itself, but another angle to it. It has to do with the either/or choice that is still hanging over women: love or career. Can a woman really do a good job at both? It's a loaded question because the implied answer is no, not unless she's Superwoman, and who wants to live with one? When the woman runs into a conflict and feels she has to throw in the towel (tea towel? jogging towel? crying towel?), does that mean that love and work are incompatible? Or is it her husband who has become incompatible?

It's possible. Studies (do they never stop?) reveal that a man can be jealous of his wife's work, particularly if she makes more money than he does – fortunately for him, this doesn't happen very often. He likes the money his wife brings in, but he also likes to have her there when he needs her, ready and waiting and welcoming and attentive and nurturing, because it's a jungle out there, and he doesn't want to hear about her jungle. I'm just telling you what I read. Now I'll tell you what I think.

I think that if two people are friends (and I hope you married one), then they share jungles the way they share everything else, because it's interesting. (See friends, page 197.) They want to hear, they want to make suggestions, to support, to cheer, to commiserate, to help each other. If either of them doesn't then they married the wrong person. ("You're not my friend, you're my husband/wife.")

If a man feels threatened by his wife's success, he should ask himself why, instead of dumping guilt on her, or accusing her of being unfeminine, or denying sex (men do it, too, in more subtle ways than headaches). Marriage is not a competition. Marriage should be the source of ease, not stress. You can get stress anywhere.

Let's at least face the ghost of guilt that haunts every working mother. She thinks she's damaging her children, taking away their right to her full-time mothering. That was a fifties myth, the one I cut my children's teeth on. We had our demands of perfection laid on us, too. Very few, if any, of us gave our children our undivided attention, even though we were home with them. Quality time, as they say, is quality time. A really good day-care system would do wonders for most young mothers' guilt, and an efficient cleaning woman would take care of the rest.

Family Stress

Family stress is different from busy-ness stress because it has to be dealt with, not merely eased or covered over. Most families can't avoid stress by one or other or both of the parents quitting or taking a lower-status job. (There *is* no lower-status job than a parent's!) Family stress is more than burnout or tiredness; it's cracks in the foundation. You can't treat the symptoms only; you have to deal with the problems, find the cause, change the system – easier said than done. Once you're a parent you don't quit, though some people try. You can't afford to ignore the warning signals of stress in the family, not if you want to stay married and hang onto your kids.

The thing is, you're so busy, how do you notice when something is not right? You're all hurtling along, doing the best you can, coping with each (minor) crisis as it raises its head. You feel as if you're shooting ducks in a carny game: as fast as you knock one down, another one pops up. Still, if your sensors are alert, there are signs of trouble that you can watch out for.

Warning Signals of Stress in Kids

• Good behaviour. This can happen after a divorce or a death in the family or some such major emotional event. A child will become the helpmate, the strong, reliable comforter of the afflicted parent, terribly responsible, sensitive – in short, too well behaved. I have met a number of young people like this, in psychiatric units of hospitals. The unnaturally good behaviour was the child's effort to regain the parent's attention, to be "loved best," to be reassured that he or she was still valuable within the family.

• Acting out, rebelliousness. This is perhaps a more common method of attracting attention. It's another bid for help. Boys particularly, so I have observed, go this route. The devil-may-care attitude is an attempt to show that nothing bothers the kid, but it's also a plea to be stopped and listened to.

• Increased aggression. We all get angry when life deals us a staggering blow. Anger is a legitimate part of the grief process and necessary to ultimate recovery. Anger often gives us the energy we need to go on, if we focus it right. But if it takes the form of anti-social aggression, it has to be re-channelled. Unhealthy aggression can be recognized in several familiar forms:

- fights with siblings
- arguments, about everything
- absenteeism, from home, from school
- late arrivals, for dinner, for family engagements
- or even no-shows.

These are not just bids for attention but also attempts to control an environment that has become too alien and too uncaring.

- Whining. A younger child who hasn't the means to make a statement by overt physical acts can resort to whining and clinging to the remaining parent. When the bottom has dropped out of a child's life as he knows it, a desperate clutching at straws is a natural reaction.
- Poor appetite, too, can be a form of protest and not only a response to a stomach that is sending out distress signals. Such stress behaviour in (usually female) teenagers is recognized now as anorexia nervosa. It can indicate a desperate refusal to allow the body to mature, a terrible need for recognition by manipulating one's self-image, a frequently fatal method of commanding parents' attention.
- Poor sleeping habits. You don't sleep well when you're worried about something, do you? Neither do your kids. Warm milk and night-lights were invented for people, young and old, with sleeping disorders. Again, as with every other stress symptom, you have to get at the cause of the anxiety.

Do you get the feeling your children are trying to tell you something? Maybe you should pay attention.

Adult Stress

I want to focus for a moment on specifically male stress. Women may be catching up in this department, but they've still a way to go. Men are still the chief victims of stress-related heart attacks and strokes, and men still have a much higher suicide rate than women (22.8 percent of men in 1986, as opposed to 6.4 percent for women). We may get very annoyed at men but it's nice to have them around, preferably healthy and preferably home. I'm sure that some of the mid-life dumps that men perpetrate on their first wives are caused by stress. When they opt for a different (younger) wife and a different lifestyle, they're actually trying to find R&R as well as their vanished youth. So, for the sake of keeping them healthy and emotionally balanced and for the sake of keeping them, let's consider a few warning signals of marital stress:

- Husband makes critical comments in *private* on wife's cooking/appearance/child care/housekeeping/intelligence.
- Husband makes critical comments in *public* on wife's cooking/appearance/child care/housekeeping/intelligence.
- Husband is jealous of men in her life.
- He flirts with other women (or men? – sometimes homosexual men come out of the closet after years of marriage).
- He has extra-marital affair(s) – if "accidentally" overt, it's really bad news.
- He is silent, uncommunicative.
- He is unco-operative.

These may be symptoms. What is really at stake are the causes of marital stress.

These symptoms are messages from the male side to the female; let it not be assumed that wives are incapable of dealing out the stressful messages. Here are some signs of distaff distress:

- Wife makes critical comments (in public and private) on her husband's lack of sexual prowess/career failure/financial weaknesses/wimpy behaviour.
- Wife over-spends, running into debt on the charge cards.
- Wife has "headaches," (that is, denies sexual release) or shuts her eyes and thinks of Queen Victoria (some husbands have been known to develop necrophilia, proving that you can get used to anything).
- She accuses her husband of never listening and then,
- She never listens.

- She indulges in conspicuous flirtation with other men.
- She drinks too much.
- She has an affair and, more important, lets it be discovered.

These may all be symptoms. What is really at stake are the causes of marital stress.

Dixie Guldner is known throughout North America for her work as a supervisor and trainer of marriage and family-life educators. She is the former director of one of Canada's largest therapist training centres in Kitchener, Ontario, and a board member of the American Association for Marriage and Family Therapy. Guldner identifies the issues of behaviour and relationships that must be resolved by any family:

- Boundary Issues. "Art," said G.K. Chesterton, "is knowing where to draw the line." The art of family living is also knowing that, and when. Marriage vows, both the old-fashioned ones and the more modern ones in use today, in essence define those boundaries for the adult partners ("love, honour, cherish, keep self only for the other"). They broadly define the limits and issues of the union.
- Power Issues. Who makes the decisions in your family? Guldner comments that a powerful woman may have difficulty forming a relationship unless she meets an equally powerful man or one she perceives as powerful; when she does, she has to spend a lot of time working on the relationship. But power implies knowledge as well. Power without responsibility is dictatorship. Ask yourself and your spouse a few questions:
- Who knows all the birthdays, not only of the children but of the grandparents?
- Who knows how to change the furnace filter?
- Who bakes (or buys) the brownies for the school meeting?
- Who jump-starts the car? (Who left the lights on?)
- Who knows the family's allergies and plans around them?
- Who knows how to unclog the kitchen sink?
- Who keeps track of the doctors' and other appointments?
- Who cleans the paintbrushes?

- Who doesn't like brussels sprouts?
- Who darns socks? (Nobody!)

Both partners should know the answers to questions like that if both partners are going to share in the decision-making. It's a lot less stressful if one partner isn't feeling resentful of the other's lack of knowledge (or interest).

- Communication. (See communication, page 111.) It takes one to talk and one to listen (see listening, page 113), and not always the same one. There are ways and ways of communicating, of showing that you care. It's amazing how much stress a family or an individual can handle if there's someone present who cares to listen.
- Task Performance. Who does the household jobs, chores, repairs, shopping, planning, painting? When? Is the work gender-assigned? Why? Who takes the responsibility for follow-up? These simple straws can break the backbone of a marriage if there's only one camel who does all the work. Simple tasks, the doing or the neglect of them, can become power issues. This is where negotiation comes in.
- Negotiation. (See negotiating, page 103.) Give a little, take a little. Unions and management do this all the time. When negotiations break down, they call in a mediator.
- Self-esteem. Listening and communication contribute to a healthy self-image. When the people closest to you pay attention, you gain confidence. Everyone needs a little ego-massaging. You have to tell your dear ones you love them, and keep on telling them. It's nice to be told, too. Telling someone you love him or her is like having a bath: it doesn't last and you have to do it every day.
- Affective feelings. Love needs to be said, but it also needs to be shown. Let's hear it for hugs.
- Space, time, energy. As feminist writer Letty Cottin Pogrebin says, "Love and time are all we have." Well, love, anyway; you may have to search for the time.

Marital Stress – A Word to the Wives

Where is it written that the wife should feel responsible or guilty? But she does. If her husband is unhappy with her performance, behaviour, delivery, care, attention, the wife is at fault. Or the job. Love, children and work, these three, but the greatest of these is love. If she fails at that, she's going to fail at the others automatically, isn't she? It's her responsibility, isn't it?

Don't automatically assume that it is. I mean, he's grown-up, too. If you feel too responsible, it means you're taking it personally. You may not be the one to blame. He really may be under terrific pressure at work, worried about money (who isn't?), attracted to someone but fighting it (you hope he's fighting it). If you think his mood swings are all because of something you did or said, you lose control. If you start being self-conscious about everything you do or say, you lose spontaneity. This is not only your husband who's having a hard time; this is your friend (see friends, page 197). Do what you would do for a friend: be sympathetic but stay detached. And get him to relax.

Invite him out to play. Go dancing. He hates dancing. Well, then, tennis? Do something physical to help let off some steam. Sex, of course, if he's in the mood, but don't make it therapeutic. Games are fun and take your mind off everything but the trivial – yes – pursuit! Movies are still a great escape and these days as close as your VCR. Try some gourmet popcorn with an X-rated movie and see what comes up.

Cook something together, something you've never attempted – not for guests, just for you, just for fun. If you can afford it, go away for a weekend, just the two of you and pick up where you left off – how many years ago now?

Listen to him. Even if he's clammed up tighter than an oyster (you know what I mean), let him know you're still there, willing to give a nonjudgemental ear to what's on his mind. Listening is one of the lesser-known skills that mistresses offer. Because a mistress has no immediate vested interest, she can afford to be more detached than a wife, and she has time. As long as he's talking and she's listening, he won't leave. You can do that – listen. Given time, he may do the same for you. Listening is one of the best, and rarest, gifts anyone can receive or give.

This is not a course in marriage-counselling. This is a book about family. We all tend to think family is for marriage. Wrong. Family is for children. Marriage is for family. As Karen Jasper (eighth grade, Bellefonte, Pennsylvania) said, "First be sure you want to be a parent." Go back to Square One. Well, not all the way, obviously, because the children are already here. But do get your priorities straight. Deal with marital stress the way you deal with your children's stress – with attention, patience, praise, sincerity, communication, respect, affection and time.

Play hookey
Sniff the flowers.

CHAPTER TWELVE

How to Prevent Family Problems

What concerns everyone can only be resolved by everyone.
— Friedrich Durrenmatt

You think you're the only one who has problems until you talk to someone else who has problems. Not that that solves *your* problems, but it makes you feel better to know you are not alone.

There are enough broad similarities in a family's problems that I can describe a general approach to them rather than try to deal with one or two more specifically. The teenager with a good-paying part-time job who is feeling very independent and wonders why he still has to obey the rules has more in common than would seem to be the case with his little sister, who is bargaining for free-range rights on her bicycle, with his father, whose pressures at work make him feel he's justified for sloughing off some of his family duties, and with his mother, who threatens to go on strike because she feels like the drudge who has to do everything.

People want to know what to tell their children about sex, how to handle allowances, why grandparents can't understand how little time they have to visit, where they can save money in an escalating economy (theirs), and who is going to listen to them, anyway? As I say, the problems are myriad and specific, but the approach to them can be generalized and spelled out. What is really helpful is some preventive care. It's like preventive housekeeping: you stop the problem before it sets in.

Family therapist Dixie Guldner considers such prevention therapeutic and offers some methods of prevention:

- Be open to information from different members of the family. Even young ones have their insights and viewpoints.
- Try to be nonjudgemental. "I don't think parents set out to ruin a child, yet they do," says Guldner. Judgements can be destructive. Self-esteem is important at any age.
- Be open to changing rules. Rules and behaviour change as families grow up. You don't keep on cutting a child's meat for her when she's eleven years old, and you don't set an 8 P.M. curfew when she's sixteen.
- Listen. (See listening, page 113.) Too many families are guilty of what Guldner calls "selective inattention."
- Learn to negotiate. Sometimes the problem is not one of communication but of negotiation. Families have to learn to win some, lose some, to give and take – and to know the difference between giving and taking. Treaties and agreements are as important as briefs and hearings.

Another Story

I have a single friend whose teenage son has a part-time job. Recently he announced to her that he was going to skip school the next day and go "cruising" with his friends. (At least he told her. One of the sad advantages of being single is that your kids talk to you more, and you listen more.) My friend said she didn't approve of skipping school, on principle. Her son said he'd been very good, needed a break, and besides, she'd let him skip school for a swimming meet out of town, why couldn't he skip again, for R&R?

My friend told me she looked up at her son, who towered over her, and wondered what to say. "Look," she said, "I can't hit you, because you're bigger than I am."

"You never did," her son said.

"I know." She continued, "I can't stop your allowance, because you earn your own money. I can't refuse to write you a note to excuse your absence, because you're beyond that sort of thing now. I can't squeal on you, because what good will that do, and I hate squealers." She looked at him. He waited. "All I can say is, I don't like it. You must honour your commitments. Right now your commitment is to school. I'm just telling you what I think is best. You have to do what you think is best."

There was a brief silence. "I'll go to school," her son said.

That boy's decision, I think, was made years before.

Conflicts

There are lots of times when you run into headlong conflict with your children or with your spouse. You think one way, they think another. How are you going to resolve your differences and still smile at each other at breakfast tomorrow – or if not smile, at least not growl? We'll break it down again, not dealing with any specific conflict, but defining the method of approach.

How to Hold a Family Council

1. Identify the conflict.
- First you define it: one side thinks/wants soanso; the other side thinks/wants suchansuch. If necessary, write down the opposing statements on paper. (I can't do anything without paper.)
- Break down the issues involved and explore them in a (calm) discussion.
- Restate the problem as it has emerged from the opposing points of view.
- Identify your concerns and feelings about the problem.
- Allow the other side to identify their feelings. (This is different from point of view. This is where gut feelings and resentments can be aired.)
- Focus on the future. What will happen if you do this? Or this? What's the worst that could happen? Go ahead and imagine the worst scenarios you can. (The kid gets hit by a

car; your daughter gets pregnant; your son gets AIDS; your wife makes more money than you do; you get a divorce – make me cry.)

2. Communicate.

- Now is the time to *listen*. No interruptions, no second-guessing, no overruling, no patronizing. Just listen. With an open mind.
- Ask questions and listen some more. No editorializing, no defending, no arguing.
- Listen to what is not being said. Sometimes the real reasons or the real needs don't come out for fear of hurting feelings, or for fear of reprisals or punishment.
- Figure out what you can agree on. Search for a common denominator, some meeting ground, somewhere. (You both want the other to be happy – also safe; you both want this marriage to continue; you all want to survive as a family.)
- Be quiet. Stay calm. Don't blow it now. Don't say anything you'll be sorry for, nothing categorical ("you always . . ."), nothing polemical ("you're a slob/a lecher/a slut/stupid), nothing shrill (screaming is shrill).

3. Consider your options.

- Have a brainstorm session. Try to think of other solutions, compromises, or even a temporary plan of action that might work while tempers cool and you figure out what's going to happen next. Again, no judging. Take every suggestion offered and consider it.
- Consider it and be receptive. No one is allowed to say, "That's stupid" or "That won't work" or "Of all the dumb ideas."
- Offer lots of suggestions and make a list of them all.
- Be appreciative. Praise everyone for helping, for taking it seriously, for contributing, for co-operating, for taking the time.
- Especially for taking the time. Believe me, it won't take as long next time. You'll learn shortcuts. But you might want to take the time, anyway, because when's the last time you all talked like this – and listened?

4. Choose a plan of action.

- If you can't make up your mind among yourselves, you may

need to call in some outside help, someone more detached than you are. Depending on what the issue is, and the people, you may require a professional counsellor, or perhaps a teacher, your minister or rabbi, a smart (not nosy) neighbour, an in-law (an in-law is someone's parent and loves you).

- Try to be objective yourself, though. After all the preliminary discussion, it should be possible to be fairly objective and to come up with a solution to suit the situation and the people involved.
- It's not written in stone. Try it for a week or a month and see how it works. If there are problems, discuss them and refine the solution.
- Remind everyone at this point to be fair and broad-minded about it. Remember: you win some, you lose some. Make that give a little, get a little.

5. Come to terms.

- Put the agreement in writing. You can include a few whereases if you like, stating the problem, but be sure to be very clear about the proposed solution.
- Include a few escape clauses in the agreement, allowing for back-sliding, errors, or obstacles when it comes to adhering to it.
- You've put it in writing. If the document is small enough, post it on the fridge door; if not, condense it and put the key words on the fridge.
- If you decided on a trial basis – a week or a month or whatever – agree to a review board when the time is up to see how it's working.

The court is adjourned.

The strength of such a structure for family discussions is the opportunity it provides for total involvement. No one within a family can change without the whole family changing. Often one member's problem will turn out to be caused by several members' behaviour patterns. When this is recognized, then all members must agree to modify their behaviour if effective change is to take place.

The problem at hand may be something as simple as being late for school. Debbie likes to wash her hair every morning, but Alex always beats her into the bathroom, so she's late. Negotiations and the posting of a schedule (on the bathroom door instead of the fridge door) may resolve the problem, but both parties have to change. Perhaps D. will wash her hair every other morning, or get up earlier; maybe A. will get an electric razor and shave in his bedroom; maybe the family will install another bathroom – or move! (This is why I didn't want to get into specifics.)

Tender Testimony

I have described the techniques for a full family discussion. Obviously, some negotiations must be limited to the members immediately involved, with maybe a mediator or two (both parents). Some testimony is too tender and personal to be heard by all, and too shattering for both parties to have it aired. Sex, drugs, divorce threats – all must be handled with tact and respect for one's privacy. However, the approach is the same and will provide a framework for constructive discussion. If the family has been accustomed to dealing with problems in this way, then the mechanism is already in place and functioning and should be useful for handling larger, serious, threatening situations.

Having recommended what may sound like incredible and long-winded openness for family discussions, I do want to point out that every family has its own level of reticence, that all individuals have their safety zone of privacy. Everyone's space should be respected. Besides that, there are always subjects better left untouched. Secrets are healthy (and also quite delicious). Sociologist Erving Goffman thinks that "points of reticence" play a strong role in a healthy family:

In well-adjusted marriages, we expect that each partner may keep from the other secrets having to do with financial matters, past experiences, current flirtations, indulgences in "bad" or expensive habits, personal aspirations and worries, actions of children, true opinions held about relatives or mutual friends, etc.

And if you think that refutes the whole idea of the family council, then forget this chapter!

THIRTEEN

How to Communicate and Listen

I have found the best way to give advice to your children is to find out what they want and then advise them to do it. — *Harry S. Truman.*

You won't be able to give your children advice of any kind if you don't talk to them and find out what they need advice about. Communication is a two-way street. That's why I lumped it with listening.

Talking

Communication begins with talking, but doesn't end there. Still, it's a place to start.

> *Communication:* 1. the act or fact of passing along; transmitting. 2. a giving or exchanging of information by talking, writing, etc. (*Gage Canadian Dictionary*).

Communication skills are among the most important tools a person can have in business these days. Every company with a message provides seminars and workshops for its employees to learn these skills and pays huge sums of money to consultants who are experts not only at communicating but at communicating the skills of communicating. (It's a brave new world that has such creatures in it!) Families could use such an expert. Communicating is one of the most essential acts a family performs, within its membership (which is what I'm concerned with here) and also outside, for it is within the family unit that an individual first learns how to interact with others.

In fact, one of the concerns of the Vanier Institute of the Family, which gets concerned about these things, is what happens to this resource when families are so small as to eliminate communication skills. The Vanier people think that one-child families hardly supply the training ground for communication and negotiation skills. Co-operation begins with two; so do generosity, sympathy and compromise. All are words and qualities that require people to co-operate with, be generous to, feel sympathy for, other people, and to agree on a compromise. All it takes is two. An only child can learn everything necessary about getting along with people in a caring, communicative family. Anyone can.

Where Do You Find the Time?

That's the common question (more like a wail) when parents say they'd like to communicate more with their children but find it hard to program the time. I'm a great believer in as-you time: As you do something, do something else! For example, chatting as you do the dishes. Since dishwashers have taken away that time in many households, you'll have to find other as-you times. Families are still the repositories of rituals and traditions. (See rituals, page 131.) Somewhere in each family's set of patterns is extra time. It's not elapsed time you're looking for, it's communicating time. Think of where and how to find it.

Time-Sharing

Time, like lots of other things, is best when it's shared:
• Keep on reading aloud to your kids, even after they can read to themselves – wonderful time-sharing! If it can't be nightly, reserve it for special times. Many families reread A Christmas Carol every year; why not read a summer book as well?

- Go together on an errand, say to the store. The walk will do you both good, and you'll have time for a chat.
- When your child tells you something, listen! I've said that before and I'll say it again.
- Take the time to praise your child. Not insincere flattery, but genuine praise:
  - Be specific.
  - Don't say it unless you mean it.
  - No qualifiers or buts: "That was good, for a girl, but I wish you'd . . ."
  - No hidden agendas: "Since you're so good at this, next time why not . . .?"
  - Be enthusiastic, but not gushy.
- "Play with us for ten minutes every day" (Jake Stingle, second grade, Clearwater, Florida).
- Every once in a while, drop everything, change your plans and play hookey with your kids. The subliminal message – that you'd rather be with them – works wonders. "Parents can give things to their children or they can spend time with their children. Time is best" (Matthew Addison, third grade, Nederland, Texas).

Time, you see, is a clear form of communication.

Theories Come and Theories Go

The theory of discipline making the rounds when my kids reached adolescence said that instead of yelling at your children and telling them they were slobs (which was supposed to be a self-fulfilling prophecy) and ordering them to clean up their rooms and pick up their clothes and towels – that is, instead of saying that they were lazy or that they forgot to take their books to school – you were supposed to turn it around and communicate to them how you felt, with as little editorializing as possible. In other words, you would say, as politely as you could, without letting that cutting edge of hysteria sharpen your voice: "I hate to see those wet towels on the floor." Or, "It upsets me to see your clothes lying in a heap." Or, "I'm not happy to see the empty popcorn bowl sitting on the sofa."

Kids were supposed to respond to this dispassionate statement of your feelings by eliminating what was troubling you, namely, by picking up the towels, hanging up their clothes, cleaning up the family room. Instead, my kids would say, "Well, if it upsets you to see that stuff, don't look." Or they would communicate back, as if you were having a philosphical discussion about wet towels: "Isn't that funny. They don't bother me at all." It just didn't work. Some crafty attempts at communication don't. Your children are way ahead of you, all the time.

I met a child psychiatrist who had seven of the best-behaved children I'd ever seen. I asked him the secret of his success. "I tell them something once," he said. "Then I hit them." (I didn't believe him and I still don't.)

Another Story

I heard a story of Jen, a sub-teen girl who went to a sleep-over in a friend's back yard, in a tent, with a couple of other girls. Naturally, the boys came around to heckle and to tease, moths to the flame. The noise disturbed the girl's parents, and the father thundered down the garden as the boys ran away.

"If your boy friend was out here talking to you, I swear you'll never be allowed to see him again," he roared at his daughter, and then asked, "Was he?"

Backed into a corner like that, what could the kid say? "No, Daddy."

The hostess mother phoned Jen's mother the next day to ask what Jen had said about the boys at the party.

"No boys," Jen's mother said. "Jen gave me a blow-by-blow account of the evening and there were no boys."

Turned out Jen had omitted a few details, but she was relieved when her mother asked her about the boys, and she talked. She had simply been trying to protect her friend, at her friend's request.

The moral is: don't invite your children to lie to you. Part of the secret of listening is not encouraging lies.

Still Communicating After All These Years

Keep the lines of communication open. It may often seem as if the lines are one-way and you wonder why you bother, but you have no right to shut yours down. Some time, you never know when, the line will be open when your child needs it.

Here are four things to keep in mind to ensure communication:

First, *recognition*. Recognize a kid's self-consciousness. Some things are hard to talk about. Wait for it. Recognize the limited verbal skills. As an experiment, I once asked a teenager (not one of my own) to attempt a conversation without once using "like" as a connective. Her speech was so halting she sounded as if she were an immigrant speaking English as a foreign language. She was, it was.

So when kids have something important to say, concentrate on the content and not on the articulate quality of the speech. Very young children can be helped by telling the "story" for them. "Once upon a time," you say, "there was a little boy/girl named (your child's name) and . . ." Perhaps you've seen this technique used recently on the TV show "thirtysomething," where a child has been helped to deal with his father's departure by contributing details to a continuing story about the hero-prince (the kid) and the monsters he deals with. The monsters, of course, are projections of his fear. If you begin a story with a child and let the child take over, you will perhaps enable both of you to understand what's going on.

Try to recognize any adolescent's growing resistance to authority and try not to take it personally. Anything you say in the way of remonstrance, or even gentle caution, is going to be resisted, so don't say it. Again, remember the basic problem of articulating what's going on. Maybe you can get at it with games. (See games, page 112.)

Second, *time*. Give them time. You can't be a time-efficiency expert with your kids. One-minute management may be effective; one-minute parenting doesn't work. Make time for your children. Make it regular, write it in stone, not to be changed, and then be gracious in the giving of it, along with your undivided attention.

Third, *sharing*. Share your thoughts. Don't come on with the subliminal editorials. "You know what I admire about you?" my father used to say to my brother and me, separately. "What, what?" I'd ask eagerly. "Uh huh," my brother would say, already seeing through it.

"What I like," my father would continue, encouraged or not, "is that you can work without anyone telling you to. You just see what has to be done and you do it." My brother would nod, bored, and turn off, heading for the drug store or wherever he went. Not me. "Yes, yes," I'd say and rush off to work. I was a suck. It doesn't work with most kids. They can recognize an ulterior motive when they hear one.

Instead of editorializing, tell your kids how you feel. One of the advantages the children of single parents have over children of complete families is that they get more of that one parent's attention and share more of that one parent's thoughts (sometimes too much!). Children, especially adolescents, can be among your best friends if you let them. Single parents not only let them, they need them.

Oh, and while you're into the sharing, tell them you love them. Keep on telling them.

Fourth, *focus*. You can't take in a thing if your shutter isn't open. You have to keep an open mind. You have to stop living in the past because nothing closes your mind faster than twenty-twenty hindsight.

That was then, this is now, and things are different. *Things* are; emotions haven't changed much. If you keep an open mind, and keep on loving, then you will be able to focus on your child's concerns. Listen with an open mind, love with open hands. You know you have to let your children go some time, so give them the skills to survive when they leave.

Games People Play

One of the best survival skills is game-playing. We all play games, of course, but there are games and there are games, as Eric Berne points out in his landmark book about the games people play. Unfortunately, most games are destructive. It might be fun to play constructive, creative ones with your family. Games for fun and profit? Games for getting through the day? Most families play games on long car trips to stave off boredom. Think about games as a means of communication in your everyday life.

For example, the word game Probe, while increasing accuracy in the use of language, also affords surprising insights into people's attitudes and perceptions. Psychiatrists have used word-association tests to help them find out what's going on in a patient's head; why can't parents do the same thing, in an unthreatening way? The newer game Scruples, billed for adults, might be an interesting game to play with your young adult children. You might be surprised at how much you'll learn and at how far the acorns have fallen from your tree. The game is based on hypothetical situations, usually involving some ethical decision and resulting action. If you baulk at the game, buy The Book of Questions and launch your own ethical and moral speculations about behaviour. With either tool, you may be amazed to find out what your kids are thinking – if you listen.

Listening

That's what this is all about, isn't it, the giving and exchanging of information? After communicating comes listening, or is it vice versa? You make your wants known: you start tuning in to other people's wants.

You have to listen to yourself as well as to others. Listen to yourself to find out if your reaction is valid or exaggerated, whether your sensitivity is justified or too hyper. If possible, get an outsider to listen and tell you. It needn't be a counsellor; it could be a friend, preferably impartial. Then listen to the others (again) and try to listen to what they're telling you, not just what they're saying. It's not easy, given your own emotional involvement. Realize you're not alone; every family has its problems. Speak directly, ask some direct, but not threatening questions. But ask yourself first if this isn't just another way to get some kicks. Don't make it just another ploy; don't confront just for the sake of confronting.

How to Listen to Your Children

The Strommens, along with every other child psychologist you'll ever read, say in *Five Cries of Parents* that it's very important to *listen* to your children. According to the Strommens, a lot of parents make mistakes in their listening. They listen with half an ear. Or they say "yes, but . . .," or "you should have done this . . .," or "you think you've got troubles, listen to mine!"

Hey! You're supposed to listen with your *heart* .

Three Guides to Listening

1. Listen in ways that encourage expressions of feeling. Be interested, nonjudgemental; keep your criticism to yourself. Make nice, affirmative noises: "uh huh," "mmmmmm", "go on," "I see what you mean." Give general leads instead of asking too sharp, too pertinent or too specific questions.

2. Try to discern your child's (adolescent's) perspective. Make an effort to know their inner life and feelings. Show that you're trying to understand: "Is this what you mean?", "Is this what you're trying to tell me?" Ask for clarification.

3. Approach each conversation with a sense of hope. You have faith in this kid. Show it.

I'll add one of my own:

4. Listen to what the child doesn't say. Or anyone, for that matter. People often don't answer direct questions, not even simple ones like "Do you want a cup of coffee?" So listen to what they're not saying. When they say, "I don't want to put you to any trouble," that means yes (please). You know that already? Well, it's the same with your kids. Listen to how they don't say what they're really saying.

How to Turn Your Child Off

1. Invite the kid for a heart-to-heart talk. Turn on the TV to your favourite show or football game, as the case may be. Adjust the volume upward. Now turn to the kid, keeping an eye on the screen and say, "What do you want to talk about?"
2. When the kid starts to tell you something, interrupt five times. Be sure to keep count.
3. Look at your watch three times. Be accurate. Count the times.
4. When the kid gives up and leaves the room, shout, "How come you never want to talk to me?"

How to Guarantee Complete Lack of Communication

Here's a list of phrases and sentences you should memorize to guarantee misunderstandings between the adult members of the family:

1. I don't want to start anything.
2. Don't go starting anything.
3. It was you who started this.
4. I know I have my faults, too, but not like yours.
5. No wonder your family is nuts.
6. No wonder your dad beat/left you.
7. Don't you talk about my family like that.
8. Do I have to hear that sob story again?
9. I've told you a hundred times already . . .
10. You're so stupid you couldn't find your way down a one-way street in a one-horse town.
11. You're taking it all wrong. Can't you take a joke?
12. What do you mean by that crack?
13. I'm fed up to the eyeballs with your nagging/whining/bullying/complaining/yelling/crying/drinking.
14. What did you say? I wasn't listening.
15. I'm not mad, dammit!

From there it's an easy misstep to a full-fledged fight. "Never go to bed angry," Phyllis Diller said. "Stay up and fight."

CHAPTER FOURTEEN

How to Make a Sandwich

They launch, and they come home again. — *Rachel Schlesinger*

The human young are unique in the animal world for the length of time they require to mature and function independently of their parents. These days it takes even longer because even when you think they're off your hands they're not. They come home again. No one reads Thomas Wolfe these days.

Fifty Plus

Everyone (read: sociologists) talks about the Empty Nest Syndrome and how hard it is on parents, especially mothers who are supposed to consider themselves out of a job. Hah! Most women I know who have reached this stage are delighted to get the kids off their hands. This is what Freedom 55 is all about, and all the early-retirement plans. This is why travel agents have lowered their special senior-citizen rates and excursions to include anyone fifty-five (sometimes fifty) and over. This is the target market of the successful American magazine, *50 Plus*. This is called Afternoon Delight, as opposed to the Twilight Zone, when you start losing your friends, your teeth and your marbles. All you've lost is your children, and they still come round at Thanksgiving and

Christmas. Only now they don't seem to know enough to stay away the rest of the time. By the last census, there were over a million children over the age of eighteen living at home with their families of origin. So you see, you're not alone. If the trend continues, no one will be.

Social Reasons

Dr. Robert Glossop has listed the most significant reasons for this social phenomenon (with my comments):

- Education. It takes longer to get one these days, but without it there's small hope of being financially independent. In the meantime free room and board at home is very handy.
- The economy. The kid might have a job, but not one of your top exec slots. In fact, the remuneration is quite modest, not to say meagre, and rents are not. I have a friend in Connecticut whose son commutes to New York City to work because accommodation in the city is scarce and dear. The same is true in most large cities where singles are the fastest-growing segment of the population and single-dwelling units are the most in demand. As for houses, they cost the price of a kid. So the kid stays home.
- Unemployment. Just because they have a job doesn't mean they will keep it. The unemployment rate in the early-to-mid-twenties is three to four percentage points above the overall rate. This is part of the hazard of being a Boomer: too many people, not enough goodies to go around. When they lose their jobs, they can't afford to pay rent, so they come home.
- Marriage postponement. According to StatsCan, the average age of marriage in 1985 was 24.6 years for brides and 26.7 for grooms. That's up by two years from 1975. So as long as they're not married, and rents being what they are, they might as well stick around, right?
- Birth to unwed mothers. One survey concluded that about half of all unwed mothers take their babies home for at least the first two years. I have told this story in another book, of the young unmarried woman who brought her baby home for her mother to care for while she went back to finish her education. The girl's parents were just on the point of

retiring, looking forward to freedom and travel, and now they're stuck with another child. I had a friend who used to tell her kids when they came to her with homework problems: "You do it; I passed Grade Four." That's what this woman should tell her daughter: "I passed Night Feeding One – a long time ago." She doesn't say it, of course; no one ever does. Once a parent, always a parent.

- The high divorce rate. In my day, going home to mother used to be a joke. Now it's no joke.
- The declining remarriage rate. I don't buy this one, actually. The remarriage rate is higher now than the first-time marriage rate. But certainly *between* marriages, home is a nice place to go, especially if there are children and you can get free baby-sitting, too. That's what grandparents are for, right?

Most parents now are finding it necessary to set a time limit on the return to the nest. As one grandmother put it, referring to the night-time crying of her grandchild, "I can't take that any more. I don't have the patience." You don't, either. You had enough togetherness the first time around to last you a lifetime.

You don't mean that. No one heard you say it. You love your children. You love to have them visit. The key word is *visit*. It's when they come to stay that it gets hard. They're too big to control, too independent to hit in the curfew or pocketbook, too *alien*.

There's another side to this, of course. Think how these kids feel, and if you're one of them, you have my sympathy. I'm old enough, you see, that I've experienced both sides.

My Story

We did it to my parents. We had two children and were ready to move into a house when our mortgage arrangements fell through and we had to build a house, which wouldn't be ready for six months. We had already given notice on the duplex we were living in and we had no place to go. We moved in with my family of origin. Suddenly I was the child of my parents, dependent again. Though I had been married and running my own household for six years, I stopped thinking. I couldn't plan meals, I didn't seem to function the same. Sex, need I say, was difficult; I felt virginal, guilty and afraid to make any noise.

Manitoba's liquor laws had just changed, and Winnipeg got licensed bars that summer. My husband and I tried them all, one by one as they opened, celebrating the framing in, the wiring, the plastering, every stage of our house as it became ready to receive us and taking the opportunity to get out of the parental house to be free to talk – leaving free baby-sitters behind, mind you.

I was in an apartment when it happened to me as a parent, and though it was only for a brief time, it felt like Tobacco Road or slum living while we went through it. My youngest was still at home, had never left; my next youngest lived at home while working at his summer jobs between university years – so that was only four or five months, but there was an overlap because my next up returned broke from Europe and I gave her room and board until she got a job and a stake. Suddenly I was planning big meals again, juggling other schedules than my own, handling more laundry and finding the voice I thought I had forgotten how to raise. I had one advantage, if you want to call it that: I was widowed, and I really enjoyed my children's company.

There's still another aspect to this extended family trend, and that is the dependency of aged parents. More and more frequently now, as people's life expectancies increase, parents are outliving their money and their strength and cannot live alone. Old couples can manage longer, though you'll hear of cases where both are too frail to cope and must be separated in nursing homes. Usually, however, an aging, widowed mother requires a home and people to care for her. Guess who?

That's why professor Benjamin Schlesinger calls these forty- to fifty-year-olds, parents of children and children of parents, the Sandwich Generation, layered as they are between the needs and dependencies of the older and the younger generations surrounding them. Even if their aging parents live apart from them, they have needs (and demands) that must be met. Even if their worried children finally leave the nest, they still need support, if only (!) emotional.

As always – one of the major refrains of this book – keep the lines of communication open.

Some Things to Consider

Robert Glossop thinks maybe what's been happening is a sign that we're moving toward more dependence on family units. Think about it. Here, adapted from the *Toronto Star*, are a few questions to start you talking before you all move in together:

- Are you going to pay rent? How much?
- Are you going to plan meals and eat together? Who's paying for the groceries? Who's cooking? Who's washing up?
- Who's going to do the laundry?
- Is the boarder going to be a child or parent, a tenant, or an adult responsible to other people in the household?
- And for heaven's sake, if you're a vegetarian, get your own tofu!

Grandparents

Grandparents are younger than they used to be, but they're going to be older. That is, people are staying young and active longer, but they're also living longer, so they're going to have a long old age. This development is what has led to the problems of the Sandwich Generation. Let's take a look at a few statistics to see what we're talking about.

The Stories Stats Tell

In the next forty-five years the older population (people sixty-five or older) is expected to triple. The number of older older people (those seventy-five and over) is also expected to triple. No one expected the numbers to be this dramatic, least of all the people who are aging. As Eubie Blake said on his one hundredth or so birthday, "If I'd known I was going to live this long, I'd have taken better care of myself." Women, of course, outnumber the men. In 1986 for every 100 men between sixty-five and sixty-nine years, there were 125 women in that age bracket; for every 100 men aged eighty to eighty-five years, there were 175 women.

One futurist has suggested that the way to get around the imbalance of male-female population in the upper age range would be to institute polygamy – for one man to have two or more wives. (I know, I think so, too.) Quite apart from any moral objections you might have (there have been some rigidly moral religious sects, as you know, that have practised this custom), you know that it wouldn't work at all. Women share kitchens even less well than they share men.

But what do we do? Once we women reach a certain age, nothing seems to stop us except rot. Men, I'm happy to say, are living longer, too. Their life expectancy is actually rising faster than women's now, though it hasn't quite caught up. Both sexes are surviving longer at the top ages. The question is, are they still part of the family system?

Married women living with their husbands comprise 36 percent of the female population aged sixty-five and older, while 70 percent of men that age are heads of households. Ay, there's the rub. The general indication is that men who survive do so in a married context (and if they are widowed, they marry again); women who survive go on alone. But we are not yet a nation of institutions. A very low percentage (under 10 percent) of our old people live in institutional homes. The majority of older single people live with one or more relatives, either blood- or marriage-related – in other words – family. But we have seen the future and it is us. You and me. Be warned.

If you're a Sandwich Filling, you're already into it, helping to care for your own parents and stockpiling for your long future. If you're younger than that, you know that you and your peers will be part of that huge Age Boom that those coming after you will be unable to support, so you, too, are preparing for the long evening ahead. Put down your Horchow Catalogue for a minute and take a long look at your retirement plans.

The Disappearing Grandparents

The most pressing present problem is what is happening to grandparents when there is a divorce in the family. Just because a mate has been exed doesn't mean the grandparents have to disappear. But that is often what happens. One or other side of the family sinks into oblivion. That's not only unfair to the children; it's heart-breaking to the grandparents. When it comes to divorce, people take very short views; they think they're dealing with two generations. They're not. Several generations may not live under one roof any more (they seldom did), but that doesn't mean that the extended family network isn't just as important as it ever was, perhaps even more so when there is a hole in the net. It might be wise, in the case of divorce, to make sure the children get custody of the grandparents.

Everyone needs nurturing, especially children and especially children from split families. Whether the grandparents are the ex's parents or the custodial parent's parents, they must be remembered and loved, and they'll do the same. Keep including them in family gatherings and let them know family news and events. Encourage the children to keep in touch with their grandparents. A member of that older, wiser generation may be able to give your child some sense of security, an assurance of continuing love, a scrap of insight into their parents' lives. When the world as they knew it has come crashing down around their Walkmans, teenagers especially may find a grandparent a very real source of comfort and understanding. If not for the sake of the old ones, then for the sake of the young ones, don't separate them. Continue to allow them access to each other, no matter whose parents the grand ones are.

We need all the nurturers we can get.

Helping Hearts Grow Fonder

In the case of geographic absence, try to make the distant relatives seem close. (Why do you think those ads for long distance phone calls are so poignant?) Apart from that twentieth-century wonder, the phone, there is also a little thing called a tape recorder. I know grandparents who tell or read their grandchildren stories on tape and mail the cassettes.

Speaking of stories, that's one of the things grandparents are supposed to be for. Even ones who are not gifted at story-telling can enthrall a young child with stories of the "olden days." If nothing else, it gives the child a sense of personal history.

I met one grandmother, not a writer, who was making it the last work of her life to describe one day in her life. This is not as simple as it sounds. She had been working on it for about three years when I met her, and she was only up to midmorning. She is describing and explaining everything: decor, texture, assumptions, habits, sources and so on. It took her pages, she said, to describe the bed and its fittings: sheets, pillows, electric blanket, mattress, box spring (without using your hands, explain a water bed) and so on. That's a very detailed kind of storying. That woman's "Day" should be a useful social document, not only for her grandchildren but for historians in the future.

What About You?

You also need nurturing. Sooner or later that twilight zone is going to envelop us all. You should be considering your own faltering steps toward rocking-chair country. This Big Boom generation is quite precarious about the future, and with good reason. There are so many Baby Boomers that, by the time they reach retirement, there will be more people drawing old age pensions than there are in the work force supporting the plans. It wouldn't hurt to give a thought to your own old age while you still have your wits about you and some chance of making economic sense of it.

I hear a lot of people, younger than myself, who are now struggling to take care of their long-lived parents, declaring emphatically that their kids aren't going to have to look after them, that they're going to stay independent in their old age. (It's a good thing they feel that way, because they don't have enough kids to fall back on anyway.) Yet these same people are part of the consumer generation, the ones who are into Sunday brunch and VCR movies every weekend, the right clothes for every occasion, take-out food, rental yentls, and a well-deserved break of some kind every day. Where's the money for the future when the present is so expensive?

Have a Plan

It's money time again, and time to talk. Again, you have to agree on your goals so you won't sabotage each other. And you have to pay yourself first if you're going to save for a nest egg, keeping in mind that the egg has to be bigger than it used to be because you're going to live longer than your forebears. Define what you really want, and then figure out how much you're going to have to give now to get it later. You'll find you have to come to emotional terms with your self as well as to financial terms.

There's lots of information out there, and lots of plans (annuities, RRIFs, pensions), also lots of advice in newspapers, magazines, books (I wrote one on retirement planning) and people. Do some reading, some exploring, shop around for information, maybe even engage a financial planner (there are lots of them around, too), and figure out how and where you're going to live at the end of the rainbow. If you're going to be a worry-free grandparent yourself, you may have to begin now.

CHAPTER FIFTEEN

How to Have a Productive Dinner Time

After a good dinner, one can forgive anybody, even one's own relatives. — *Oscar Wilde*

More than 40 percent of the food dollar is spent outside the home now, on restaurants, fast food and take-out. Seven percent of Americans eat at McDonald's each day. McDonald's accounts for 11 percent of all meals in North America and 25 percent of all breakfasts. I found this frightening until I heard (on CBC) the results of a new survey: six out of seven main meals are still eaten at home, and three times a week they are complete meals – a full, cooked dinner, not just reheated leftovers (there's nothing wrong with leftovers!) or snacks. I presume this Canadian survey didn't count lunch, because no one is home.

Dinner Time!

At least three times a week you have a chance to make it as a family. How long does it take you to eat? In a group, twenty minutes to an hour, depending on the quality of the conversation and what's for dessert. Now's your chance. You've got three hours a week to be together without outside distractions, to share your news, hopes, disappointments, to solve each other's problems, to listen, to communicate. This is what family is all about. Family is more than a bunch of statistics; family is human beings in action. Where better to see them in action than at table? What do we see? What do we learn?

RULES AND MANNERS

(or not, as the case may be):

- Don't lean the side of your arm on the table.
- Don't talk with your mouth full.
- Stop poking your sister with your fork.
- No phone calls or TV during meals.
- Don't shovel your food in without chewing.
- Stop kicking your brother.
- You eat like a pig.
- How many times have I told you to ask, not stretch?
- Please pass the salt (easy on the sodium), butter (watch out for cholesterol), bread (make sure it's fibre-full).
- Eat your spinach or you don't get any ice cream. (Bribery, coercion) and an unintentional editorial about the relative merits of spinach and sugar.)
- Don't tease the baby.

TABLE CONVERSATION:

- So what did you do at school today? (Interrogation as an attempt at companionship.)
- You did what???
- A funny thing happened on my way to the office . . .
- Can I have the car on Saturday night?
- Is that really dead roast cow (or pig or chicken)? (This from your first fledgling vegetarian.)
- I'm just not hungry.
- We will now discuss a) junk food, b) eating between meals, c) anorexia nervosa.

SEX ROLES AND THE FAMILY:

- Why do I always have to clean up and never him?

- Listen to your father.
- Don't be rude to your mother.
- Sit still, I'll get the coffee. (Who said that?)

I know a kid who was assigned a school project on the interaction of his family. He set a tape recorder under the dining room table, and the results were a revelation – not to the teacher, but to the family. Why not be your own tape recorder and listen to what's going on? This is assuming that there is some doubt in your mind about the quality of your dinner table (not the food, the conversation) and some desire to improve it.

Tips for Creative Mealtimes

Here are some suggestions for using table time effectively.

- Discuss politics. Kids who are bored can leave the table but those who stay can listen, ask questions, get answers. My husband used to test us to see if we could name all the premiers of the provinces and their parties (I can't do it any more).
- Discuss business. These days there's a lot to discuss: free trade, the stock market, father's or mother's problems at work.
- As the kids get older, pick a subject (capital punishment?) and discuss it thoroughly. Get everyone's opinion and beat it into the ground. Take a look at The Book of Questions to get you going on some wild conversations.
- Report on the day and maybe make a story of it? My father was a doctor, as I've told you. After listening to others' complaints all day he just wanted the good news please, so we had to report amusing events, happy endings, and personal triumphs. (I'm not recommending to anyone that they require their children to justify their existence each day.)
- Listen to the others, and remember what's going on. Then you can follow up on what happened the week or day before: How did the test go? Did you get your report in on time? Did you settle that disagreement with Charlie?
- Play quiz show. My family did this for years. My father was a

mine of miscellaneous information, especially geography. We were way ahead of *Trivial Pursuit*. My kids hated quizzes, but we played games after dinner.

- I used to like going around the table asking for a response to a question or a punch line to a situation until I found a *New Yorker* cartoon of a woman doing that and I decided I sounded like an amateurish talk-show hostess.
- Clean-up time often sends sex signals. So does cooking time. I know two married men, a decade apart, who do all the cooking in their households. My husband, as the years passed, took on equal time. He was excellent at cooking meat-it all started with the barbecuing-but as the years went by, he elbowed me away from the stove.

Events of the World and Other Places

I will never forget the night of the Great Brussels Sprouts Mutiny. Our children put their forks and their feet down simultaneously and refused ever to eat brussels sprouts again, and my husband and I agreed with them. Never had we experienced such unanimity as a family! The kids tried it again a few weeks later with another kind of sprouts-bean, this time-but I reserved some rights. Thin ends of the wedge (or sprouts, as the case may be) could in time lead to boycotting of an entire food class, if one is not careful. The point is that the dinner table is almost the only place where the entire family is sometimes together. Use the time, and the food, well.

Comfort Food

I've already referred to comfort food, the simple, comforting food of your childhood, often served when you were sick. The food was usually heavy on the carbohydrate, but quite bland, milky, or eggy, salt or sweet, about equally divided. Chicken soup we have already mentioned, custards and milk puddings, toast (but sometimes intricately cut, as into "soldiers" or small triangles, and no crusts), pasta-all these are someone's comfort foods. Recently a friend invited me for dinner and served me his special comfort foods: macaroni and cheese, with applesauce and brussels sprouts. (I didn't tell him.) I leave you to explore your own memories of comfort food, and then to deny, if you can, the power of the family table.

Junk Food

To many kids (and some adults) today junk food is supreme comfort. Junk food is what Couch Potatoes love best: seven different flavours, cuts, thicknesses and shapes of potato chips, five varieties of pretzels, multiflavoured popcorn with imitation butter, white bread slathered with hydrogenated peanut butter, nachos and cheese (a recent entry), sugar-coated cereal, and any drink that ends in -ade and doesn't have nerdies in it (some food manufacturers add lumps to fruit-flavoured drinks to give them "mouth feel," but they should know better).

Junk food has nothing to do with the family at table. It is the enemy of quality and nutrition and of family unity. It increases the number of food contacts (as the food experts call them) per day to about twenty, as opposed to the old-time three squares, and reduces people contact. I know a lot of families that rarely eat together. Breakfast, if taken, is solitary, standing up and being sure to wash your bowl and spoon (cereal), or plate and knife (toast and peanut butter). The midday meal is the same: a sandwich in the hand is cheaper than McDLT at the corner, and who has time for fabricated family fun at lunchtime? Dinner is often snacks if everyone eats on the run (we're getting perilously close to discussing lifestyle). So the cook(s) rely on the freezer, the microwave (46 percent of Ontario homes have microwaves now, and counting; 76 percent of American homes have them), convenience, processed and engineered (read: synthetic) foods.

The Family at Table

The metaphor for the planetary community, to replace the old image of men on horseback riding around the planet keeping us all in order, may be that of the family at the dinner table: the world family at the world dinner table. The family at the table is a basic human metaphor of sharing. — Elise Boulding

Breaking bread together is a wonderfully human, intimate thing to do. Nurturance begins at the table but does not end there, nor is it a solely female task, though we have (mistaken-ly) assigned it exclusively to women in the past. Granted, the preparation and serving of food are complex acts. Divorced men find it one of the biggest challenges of single fatherhood. Perhaps this is one of the reasons so many families eat only three dinners at home a week.

Early feminist Charlotte Perkins Gilman in her book *Women and Economics* (published in 1898) commented that "a family unity which is only bound together with a table-cloth is of questionable value." These days we're lucky if we get place mats, but there's no doubt about the value of the dinner table.

CHAPTER SIXTEEN

The Importance of Rituals

You don't start traditions, traditions start. — *Skinnell's Rule*

Every family knows about rituals. Rituals are why airlines make money and people go broke getting home for Thanksgiving, Christmas, the "holidays," attending family weddings, baptisms (yes, they still have those), bar and bat mitzvahs, anniversaries and funerals. Rituals illustrate better than anything exactly what family is about: growth, process, change. They provide what Robert Glossop calls lines of demarcation, by which we can measure and observe growth and change. It's what I call door-frame reckoning. You can buy them now: fancy long fold-out paper charts with the years printed on them to enable his parents to see how little Billy has grown. In my day we used a door frame. Every summer when we went to our cottage at the lake we would back up against the pencil marks on the door frame to see how much we had grown in a year. That's a line of demarcation. That's what ritual is about.

Tradition

I'm writing this chapter two days before Christmas. (Did you know that 9 percent of Jewish households in America have Christmas trees? My Jewish friends call them Hanukkah trees.)

Like everyone else at any festival time, I am overwhelmed by memories of past festivities. Christmas, Easter, Hanukkah, Passover – most major annual events are almost nothing but ritual, on whatever level (religious, familial) you care to look at it. The worship, the songs, the food, the tree, the candles, the gifts – all are part of a comfortable, comforting accumulation of memories. As procreative families are formed, they must absorb and assimilate the traditions of their families of origin and create (slightly) new traditions and rituals of their own. I've been watching my children do this, and it's fascinating to see new rituals being formed and old rituals being adapted and changed.

Some families let Santa decorate the tree when he comes; others do it together before the big day; still others have a tree-trimming party with their friends and friends' families. Some Santas wrap all the presents and leave them under the tree; others leave a display of gifts, all unwrapped; still other Santas fill the stockings and that's all. Some families have their big celebration on Christmas Eve; others wait till Christmas Day. Not only does the procreative family have to work out all these details but it also has to deal with two families of origin. Patriarchs die hard. As long as my father was alive, we were expected to go to my parents' home (my husband had no parents to compete); when my father died, my mother came to us. My children's father died early, so again there is no competition from one family of origin – a sad convenience. I do different things every year, depending on what seems to be appropriate for my children.

What do you do? Consider your activity in the context of your life cycle and your family's. You will probably discover that you are bound not only by tradition but also by time – yours and other people's.

I have Jewish friends who added more tradition to their lives than their parents gave them: one who created a Succoth house for her kids every year, another who makes (very tough!) Hamentashen, and one who travelled a lot with her children and who used to drive room service to distraction with her request for glass dishes (as an approximation of separate plates) and special food orders as she tried to adhere to the dietary restrictions of Passover in a hotel room.

Different Strokes

Here are some things that people I know consider an essential part of their Christmas ritual:

- A wind-up mechanical toy (the man who told me he expects this is now forty-one years old!).
- A Japanese (mandarin? clementine?) orange in the toe of the stocking.
- Cookies and milk set out for Santa Claus.
- Charades and parlour games after Christmas dinner.
- A Christmas concert in which a) the children perform, b) everyone performs – recitations, songs, a joke, whatever, c) professionals perform – either on stereo or TV (How many times have you seen *The Wizard of Oz*?).
- Christmas crackers, and wearing your paper hat throughout the meal. (This is a British-Canadian custom; my American son-in-law and his family never heard of it until I arrived for Christmas dinner.)
- Candles (there are so many rituals about candles, I leave you to think of yours).
- The food, of course – the "sacrificial meat" – and the ritual trimmings.
- The decorations: the ratty or glamorous or antique, artistic, significant, sentimental, innovative, stereotyped collection of ornaments that go on the tree each year and get stored with memories to be brought out again the following year, successively shinier with the patina of love and time.

What's So Bad About Roll Call?

Best-selling pop psychologist Wayne Dyer (*Your Erroneous Zones, Pulling Your Own Strings,* etc.) endeared himself to the Me Decade by telling people they didn't have to dance to others' tunes. He said you don't have to be subject to your family's "roll call." If you'd rather be in Florida at Christmas than with your preachy parents, snotty sister and boozy brother, then go ahead, no one's stopping you. No *one*, maybe, but a lot of *things*, like tree ornaments and tradition, and maybe even your own conscience.

What's wrong with roll call? There are times when other people really are more important than you are, and ritual family times are most of them. Personally, I like to be the kind of person you can count on at roll call. I try always to be there for my family, and you should, too, for yours. That's why airlines will never go broke at Christmas. It's not the trips to Florida that are keeping the planes in the sky. It's families.

Other Ritual Times

As for the rest of the calendar year, Hallmark and the other card companies would also go broke if we didn't have such a respect for ritual. You can find a card to celebrate almost anything and to remember almost anybody, from new homes, new jobs, trips, retirement, divorce and menopause to aunts, uncles, grandparents, stepmothers, live-ins, lovers and secret pals. I've seen cards for vasectomies. Soon, I'm sure, there will be cards for artificial insemination donors and surrogate mothers. Of course, anniversaries go on forever, it goes without saying.

Anniversaries do *not* go without saying something. Heaven help the husband who forgets the anniversary of his marriage; jokes may be made about it, but marriages can founder on it. (It's a symptom, not a cause.) Letty Cottin Pogrebin offers a list of disparate items to determine whether either party is a "partner or a boarder." The list includes knowledge of grandma's birthday. (Whose grandmother?) Let me add children's birthdays and special events: music recital, church pageant, school play, field day, swim meet and so on. Both parent-partners should remember and honour them. Year by year these events take on some of the trappings of ritual. Even report-card-signing has a quality of ritual about it. Attention must be paid. (You've heard that before, too.)

"All we have are love and time," Pogrebin says. Sometimes time is squeezed, as we know too well. Rituals can actually save time and distill love – especially private rituals.

Private Rituals

My father was a very ritualistic man. I will give you examples of a few rituals that he started that are continuing, if in somewhat diluted form, in several procreative families that I know. Feel free to incorporate them or to add your own from your private store. If nothing else, this will release your memories.

- Happy First-of-the-Month. Not just Happy New Year, but Happy New Month. There's a kind of game involved here: first one to remember what day it is and to wish the others Happy First-of-Whatever wins. The prize is its own reward. Larks tend to win over nightingales in this ritual, but you'd be surprised how many hours of a day can pass before you remember it's the first of the month. No big deal, but if you like beginnings, you get twelve a year instead of just one. But I just learned of a family who celebrates the second of the month, for similar reasons. And I know a couple of families who have a member with a birthday on the thirteenth. Inevitably the event will take place on Friday the Thirteenth. So these families are rigorous about celebrating all thirteens, to ward off bad connotations and evil spirits.

- Birthday Parade. The person whose birthday it is stays in bed, pretending to sleep. The other members of the family get up a little earlier, gather together and parade in to the Birthday Person singing the birthday song and bearing loot. To wake up like that once a year, convinced that you are the most important person in the world and that your presence means a lot to other people, is a wonderful feeling. (In the case of small families, one has to use some ingenuity to make a parade.) When I moved into Toronto with the boys after my husband Bill died, Liz and Kate both showed up at 7 A.M. for John's first birthday in the new place, Liz from residence at York University on the outskirts of the city and Kate from residence at Wilfrid Laurier University at Waterloo, sixty miles away. Never underestimate the power of ritual!

- T.L.s. Does anyone else know about Trade-Lasts? A Trade-Last is something nice someone else said about a member of your family and you offer it to that person *after* he or she tells you something nice a third party said about you. You can't get off by saying you think your sister's backhand is a thing of beauty or, wow, your brother is a terrific cook. You trade *last*. People often end up owing you, but you'd be surprised how they, and you, remember who owes and who's one up. You can play this with friends, too, but it's better in the family, because everyone shares in it.

- Pudding Stories. This is one of my rituals. When we went on long car trips (in the early days a long car trip was the hour and a half it took us to drive to the lake), I used to tell my children Pudding Stories. Each child was allowed to give me one "ingredient" and then I'd make up a story using the ingredients. Good training for a writer and good entertainment for the kids. I just started telling Pudding Stories to my grandchildren. I know a family with an only child that allows the child three ingredients.

- And then there is pumpkin-carving, and Easter-egg-dying, and cinnamon hearts in the applesauce, and toasting marshmallows on the fall bonfire, and all those things you never thought of as ritual, but they are.

- There are also weekly routines, the most common and pleasant being Sunday brunch, before, after or instead of church. Post-church brunches usually start with Mimosas these days (equal parts champagne and fresh-squeezed orange juice), but lots of people like a little ting in their Tang earlier than that. Even men who do no other cooking will prepare breakfast on Sunday, and each has his specialty. I know one man who cooks sourdough pancakes for his family on Sunday morning, another who makes the most wonderful (fattening) home fries. One family creates crêpes – well, the crêpes are the same, but the fillings vary according to the whim of the creator. I've put my recipe for Buttermilk Pancakes in the appendix for those who want to start their own Sunday ritual with a good one.

That's How It Was

What I'm going to tell you next is not quite ritual but a useful tradition that my father began. I still do it for myself, privately. At the end of some event – it could be the end of each day on a car trip, or the end of summer holidays, or the end of exams, or of a school election (that I lost), or, later, the end of a college romance, my father would say, "Let's summarize what happened, and what we/you accomplished." Then he'd go on to point out that we had driven five hundred miles and crossed three state lines, or that I had earned a swimming badge, or passed another milestone on the highway of education (people used to say things like that in those days, not just my father), or that I'd learned a lot from that boy – and my father seemed to know how much! And I'd nod and say, "Yes, yes, that's how it was," and it was as if he had given me my experience to hold and keep forever.

He did the same when he was dying, of cancer of the liver. The terminal illness was brief, as illnesses go, but it gave my father enough time to summarize his life, as if to say "This is what I learned, and this is what dying is like." I listened, and I nodded, "Yes, yes, that's how it was." I later learned that the final, major step in coming to terms with death is that kind of acceptance.

So was that ritual or therapy?

A Short History of the Family

What we're really talking about is history. All of these rituals, traditions and memories create a living, changing history of each family as it grows and interacts and keeps on changing. The family is dynamic, an organism with a collective life of its own, separate and individual and unique unto itself. (That, of course, is why divorce can never be completely final, because memory can't be wiped out and history doesn't cease to exist.) Each family's traditions and rituals help to identify it and help it, also, to keep on growing, to add cumulative layers, like rings on a tree.

Birth and death, with confirmations and bar and bat mitzvahs and rites of passage and weddings (and divorces) in between – that's what family history is about, on and on and on, like forever. Looking at pictures in a family album, hanging the ornaments on the tree, telling stories, remembering family jokes – all these simple activities give us a handle on our family and ultimately, ideally, on our place in society and in history.

CHAPTER SEVENTEEN

Manners and Morals

The great secret of morals is love. — *Percy Bysshe Shelley*

It is not by accident that I lump manners and morals together. They both begin on a very simple level, based on the Golden Rule. Manners teach a sensitivity for others' feelings and suggest some guidelines for protecting them. Morals take over from manners for the big stuff, but it's the same thing: being responsible for and caring about other people's well-being, that is, loving your neighbour as yourself.

Manners as Guidelines

Rituals, as we have seen, are not only for the "public" rites of passage we all go through but also for private demarcations peculiar to each family. There are certain rules about public rituals, and they're usually quite useful. For example, at funerals ritual gets everyone through a lot of swampy emotional territory because we all know what to do. When people know how to behave – and ritual tells them how – they usually behave pretty well. You might call manners the guidelines for ritual. That's why manners are important.

Innate Manners

If you're lucky, you learned your manners in your family. We all know that, like it or not, our children's behaviour reflects on their parents, especially you know whom. Fathers usually take responsibility for more "important" behaviour, such as physical courage or prowess and good grades, which reminds me of a nice line of Robert Frost's: "You don't have to deserve your mother's love. You have to deserve your father's. He's more particular." I'm not sure that it's true. Anyway, you teach your children manners. What, exactly, are you teaching them? While you're at it, are you courteous to them?

Another word for manners is *etiquette*. A lot of people shy away from the word. Etiquette, they think, is for sissies and snobs, with all its la-de-da rules about when and how to curtsy and which fork to use first at a formal dinner and what to call the Queen if ever you should chance to meet. All etiquette – or courtesy, or manners – really is is consideration. Consideration means you don't eat with your hands or pick your nose in public because you might offend someone else. Somewhere along the way some of the rules got a little refined (not eating with your hands is one thing, the correct choice of forks is carrying it further than most people ever need to). You help your children a lot if you teach them the basic rules though. That's another thing families are for. They teach their members how to behave in public.

The Presentation of Self Families govern one's public presentation in many ways that we are not even fully conscious of. We should learn to distinguish the ways and to lay blame or praise where it is due without falling into yet another stereotype. That ring-around-the-collar commercial, for instance, is annoying because it assumes that it is the woman's job to keep his shirt presentable and her fault if it's not. If your kids or house are dirty, whose fault is it? And if your family doesn't behave well, who cares more? Do you share the responsibility? Unfortunately, it's still true that women control or are largely responsible for how the family appears in public (or else the collar ad wouldn't wash). Listen to some one-sided dialogue and see if any of it sounds familiar:

- "You are not leaving this house looking like that!"
- "Always wear clean underwear in case you have an accident and have to go to the hospital."
- "What's Melanie's mother going to think if she sees you wearing that ratty old sweater?"
- "You're not going anywhere until you clean up."
- "I'm not going to be seen with you until you get a haircut."
- "The least you could do is shave when we have company coming."
- "The guest towels are for the guests."
- "Please don't eat the daisies."

No matter whose responsibility it ultimately is, our families teach us what appearances to foster, what behaviour to endorse. Unspoken rules in every family somehow, without ever being spelled out, tell us what is and isn't acceptable behaviour (particularly in the areas of sexual activity and incest, the most common taboos). Apart from these general rules, most of us have been given a role to play within the family, not always realistic or consistent with the truth (as we see it). Sometimes, but not always, the role our family gives us is the first role we play in public, although it may not be the last one.

Thus, a bright girl may be required to hide her intelligence and seem less capable than she really is. A gentle boy may be forced to acquire a macho exterior to protect himself from ridicule. Fathers who know best have been allowed to think so by deceptive wives who make all the decisions and do all the work behind the scenes, giving their husbands nothing to do but approve. And klutzy women are considered wonderful mothers because they're so kind and bumbling and never critical. Present-day ideals of partnership require other performances, perhaps not yet perfected by either party.

"All the world's a stage," said Shakespeare, but we're not all players, not all the time, I *hope* not all the time. The family teaches us our first lines, that is, our manners, the learned techniques by which we get along with others. What we do with them after that depends on a number of things: discipline, luck, nerve and character.

Situational Ethics

Situational ethics is the name given to a subject that is actually being "taught" in some schools now. Hypothetical situations are presented to students, who must then decide on the appropriate response. Example: you and a group of tourists are trapped in a cave with an escape hatch through a crawl space large enough to admit one person at a time; there is enough air to last about two hours and the chance that a further rock slide will seal you in forever. Decide who goes first, and the subsequent order of escape. Other similar no-win situations are offered and demand discussion about ethical behaviour (not to say negotiation and manipulation) – behaviour that accomplishes the least harm or the most good, as the case may be. There's a game on the market sort of like this, too, called Scruples, based on the old idea, "Would you sleep with me for a million dollars?"

What else is family but a continuing series of situations? What better place, then, to learn how to deal with situational society and to make mistakes that are not (at first) irrevocable? A family situation is generally a forgiving one, if only because its members have to go on living with each other. Situational society is less forgiving. It offers very few exits. Ideally, the family allows its members, while learning about life, to try many doors. Ideally also, the family teaches its members basic morality, although some families have a little trouble these days distinguishing between being nice and being good.

Whatever Became of Sin?

Many people think sin is just an acronym for their social insurance number. The still, small voice of conscience that was supposed to prevent people from doing wrong is stiller and smaller than it ever was, and it is drowned out by all sorts of rationalization and justification:

• "Everybody does it."

- "They had it coming to them."
- "If I don't do it, someone else will."
- "I've had a hard life, I deserve a break."
- "I've been good for a long time, I need a holiday."
- "No one will notice."
- "I'll make up for it."
- And on and on.

As major deterrents to immoral behaviour, church and school have long since fallen away. According to moral tales of earlier decades, it was the memory of Mother's voice or the thought of Father's disappointment that kept people on the straight and narrow, just as in earlier centuries it was the threat of fire and brimstone that (sometimes) stopped an evil deed. (Define evil.) Now with the fears of a literal hell long allayed, and the sound of Mother's voice and Father's pronouncements as still as the small one within, what's to stop people from doing wrong, from harming society?

Right – the family. The family is still almost the only consistent source of moral education. It continues to instill some system of checks and balances in its members before they run rampant in society. The system of inculcation may begin with ritual and manners, but it culminates in morality.

As Robert Glossop has said, "We are beginning to remember that family is a stronger agent in the educational process than the schools, a stronger teacher of values than the church and a stronger influence on the socialization process of children than the media." It therefore behooves parents to realize what their values are and to figure out how to communicate them to their children and how to help their children internalize them. It seems to me that sometimes parents are more worried about their children swallowing their vitamin pills than their morals.

It really was easier when you had the church to help. A lot of parents these days figure they can teach their children morals without cluttering them up with religion. This next little item may have nothing to do with what the children learn, but another survey has indicated that more marriages last and last longer among regular church-goers. Just thought

I'd pass the information along. So where were we: What are the intrinsic and moral values you want to pass along?

We Hold These Truths

These are not a matter of personal preference; there really is a world- and time-honoured standard: certain basic, self-evident truths about human rights and dignity and freedom. There are also time-tested personal standards of behaviour that your children might as well learn, things like honesty and truthfulness (not the same thing), self-control, fidelity (keeping promises) and a sense of justice and fair play (loving your neighbour as yourself). It really does boil down to what Shelley (of all people!) said – love. As St. Paul reminds us:

> "Love is patient and kind; love is not jealous, or conceited, or proud; love is not ill-mannered, or selfish, or irritable; love does not keep a record of wrongs; love is not happy with evil, but is happy with the truth. Love never gives up: its faith, hope and patience never fail . . . these three remain: faith, hope, and love, and the greatest of these is love" (I Corinthians 13:4–13).

It's that simple, and that hard.

PART FOUR

Divorce

CHAPTER EIGHTEEN

Getting a Divorce

It takes two to destroy a marriage. — *Margaret Trudeau*

Your marriage was made in heaven, but in spite of all your efforts a divorce is the only way for both of you to survive. The roaring fights, the bitter recriminations, the queasy compromises, the armed truces, the prolonged silences, the icy politeness, the gut-searing pain – all have to end.

Reasons for Divorce

There are valid reasons for divorce. There are some people who should never have married in the first place, and for them divorce is a release. There are people who have overstepped the bounds of permissible behaviour whose mates must leave them in order to survive. Some people think divorces are made in heaven; they claim, wryly, that the happiest days of their lives were the day they were married and the day they were divorced. The question you're probably asking is, "How bad is too bad? How bad does it have to be before you can't go on?" Here are twelve major reasons Mary Kay Blakely suggests why women get divorced:

- What you expect is not what you get.
- You can't talk to each other any more.
- Life is too short to be unhappy.
- Alcoholism.
- Drug addiction.

147

- Physical abuse (one of the most valid reasons; a woman has a right to expect no male over the age of nine to hit her).
- In-law problems.
- You married the wrong person.
- You fight about money.
- You've both grown and changed at different rates.
- Society has changed its attitude and rules.
- Divorce is easier to get and no longer a disgrace.

Someone I knew pretty well was in the throes of breaking up a marriage that had looked okay from the outside. (One divorcee told me never to overestimate other people's happiness.) "What happened?" I wondered out loud to my friend. "I was just bored" was the answer. To me that's not a reason.

Couples in Crisis

Here are some of the warning signs that indicate a marriage is dying:

- Infrequent sex.
- Less affection.
- Fewer shared activities.
- Erosion of common interests.
- General malaise.
- Marital satisfactions gradually replaced by parental satisfactions (and when the kids leave, then what?).

This is where the scene changes to the lawyer's office.

Family Law

It might be worthwhile to consider briefly family law and marriage contracts. The laws are changing all the time, as legislators try to keep up with what's happening out here in the domestic jungle, but it takes them a while to catch up, and sometimes the changes are not always for the better. Take the no-fault divorce law and even-steven splits, both attempts to redress the grievances of the stringencies of the divorce system and the unfairness of winner-takes-all. A slice down the middle is not necessarily fair for either party, particularly in the case of a break-up of a second marriage. Here, each party loses half of what was rightfully his or hers from previous efforts in which the other had no part.

On the other hand, in the case of a first divorce, where the spoils may now be divided from a standing stop (as one divorcee put it), it's like dividing the assets of a factory, leaving all the income-generating machinery on one side only. When the machinery starts up again, the half without it slips back, having no source of new income, and uses up capital until it is penniless. The other one chugs along merrily. No recognition is given to the efforts of one partner in creating that income-bearing machinery (as in the case of a wife, for example, who puts her husband through medical or law school, only to have him dump her when the going gets good). Unfair, unfair.

Application of the Charter of Rights to family law will have to be examined case by case so that violations can be identified and corrected, some easily, some with a greater degree of controversy.

Support Payments

As for the support payments those single divorced mothers have been granted, they are as a rule notoriously low; they are also defaulted (between 50 and 90 percent, depending on what province you're looking at). Seven provinces now have legislation for the recovery of some of these payments, and it begins to be reciprocal (that is, extending enforcement into each other's jurisdiction). But even where the orders are enforced, the courts have applied a one-year rule – they will not order the payment of arrears beyond one year. (The same rule does not apply to creditors other than ex-wives.)

The Division of Matrimonial Property

The division of spoils at the time of marriage breakdown is a crucial issue. Ever since the Murdoch case, women's blood has been boiling, and laws have been reformed. (You remember the farmer's wife who contested the property settlement at the time of her divorce because her years of unpaid work in her home and on the family farm went unrecognized?) The

matrimonial property laws enacted since 1978 are an improve-
ment, but they've got a way to go.

In Quebec there are two matrimonial property options. A
wife can opt out of the basic settlement by signing her own
marriage contract, which will determine her property rights.
(Obviously, the husband has to sign, too.) For those who have
no separate contract, the Quebec rule is:

> Everything that spouses owned before their marriage, or
> acquired at any time by way of gift or inheritance, as well as
> personal items and tools used in their trade or profession, are
> separate properties that are not shared between them at any
> time; everything else (with the exception of pension rights) is
> shared equally between them at the time of their divorce.

Shelagh Day, president of the Canadian Human Rights
Reporter, comments that the Quebec law appears to be the
best scheme in the country.

If you think your marriage is in trouble (and even if you
don't), or if you are entering a second marriage, you owe it to
yourself and your family to do a little homework. The
Canadian judicial system, being adversarial in nature, is not
great when it comes to settling family law disputes. Inevitably,
if it comes to that, you will need a lawyer. His and hers, please.
A woman's husband's lawyer may be a friend of the family, but
he (or she) may turn out to be no friend of hers when it comes
to settling property or establishing child support payments.
We'll talk about custody later.

The High Cost of Divorce

Divorce is very expensive. You must know, as I do, husbands
who, under the old divorce laws, have been paying alimony to
their ex-wives for years and years and years. On the other
hand, you must know, as I do, absolute horror stories of
ex-wives living on welfare, in terrible debt, while their husbands continue to enjoy six-figure incomes. But it's the
children I worry about most.

This is not to say that we should do away with divorce.
There are genuinely unhappy people out there who, for the
sake of their health, their sanity or their safety should not be

living together. Divorce is the best thing that can happen to women who are victims of battering. Divorce seems to be the only solution when one partner is a chronic alcoholic. A mother is doing the right thing by taking a sexually abused child out of the reach of her father. In spite of the initial shock and pain, most people emerge from a divorce feeling better. If only the money weren't so tight.

Is There Life After Divorce?

Right now let's concentrate on survival after the fact. I offer you a bouquet of comments, gathered over years of listening to people:

- "It was like when I had mono – once the fever was over I was terribly weak, but I felt this relief."
- "I went crazy. I had to have a new woman every night to reassure me I was still attractive to the opposite sex."
- "I got really sick. All my defenses were down and I got one cold after another. I was a walking zombie all that winter."
- "I missed someone waiting for me when I got home. I put my stereo and lights on timers so there was noise and light when I came in."
- "I used to lie on the living room sofa in the dark listening to old tapes, love songs, and lie there, not crying, just numb."
- "I felt raw."
- "I was consumed by hatred."
- "I can't live with him, but I don't know how I'm going to live without him."

You can add some of your own; you may know the script.

Divorce and Death

Divorce is like death: you think it happens only to other people until it happens to you or someone close to you. On the stress scale, divorce ranks just below the death of a spouse as one of life's most stress-producing events – like being hit by a Mack truck, as Jean Kerr put it in her play *Mary, Mary*. Some psychologists now suggest that the two life events should be reversed, that divorce is harder to bear than death (it depends which side you're on). "At least," one divorced woman said to me after my husband died, "you know where your husband is."

I did not suffer divorce; I was widowed. But each case involves a death, whether of a relationship or of a person. Each case involves a terrible loss. Loss is a difficult fact of life to come to terms with. Loss is inexorable, irretrievable, unbearable, and yet you must bear it. Much of what I have said to my bereaved compatriots (it really is like moving to another country – a strange, empty one at first) applies to divorced people. Here's a distillation, for what it's worth, and it may be worth a lot.

How to Survive Divorce

- Be very gentle to yourself. Just as after a physical accident, or the death of a spouse, you are suffering from shock. You need warmth, quiet (this is not to say complete solitude; friends can help) and no sudden moves of any kind. Don't change your job, your home if you can help it, or any of your living arrangements if possible. Sometimes it isn't, I know. The very fact of destroying one household and creating two separate ones means you have probably moved, given up possessions (ah, the Great Divide !), set up shop in a new place.

- As quickly as you can, create a space of your own. You need a place to lick your wounds, a nest that's yours. It might be your bed, a favourite chair, a desk. Use it daily for what will amount to a ritual, an assigned time with yourself for combined pampering and planning. Have tea or coffee or a glass of lemonade or wine – it's the libation that's important – in a special cup or glass. Put some music on, sit down with it, relax. Then you can think.

- Write things down. I'm a great believer in paper. Get a notebook and pour out your anger, fears, bitterness, hopes, plans, whatever, on paper. Make your entries daily. It's part of your ritual. It's called a diary, but it's also a lifesaver.

- Make time for your friends. So many divorced people tell me

GETTING A DIVORCE 153

that their ex "got custody of their friends." If you force them to take sides, they will, and not always yours. Choose one trusted friend, for your emotional outpourings. Seek the others for hours to enjoy. If they continue to enjoy being with you, they'll keep calling.

Widows and divorcees both tell me that "you find out who your friends are," and that's true. If you have less money, you'll find you can't afford to keep up with your tennis-playing or partying friends, and they will drop you. (You'll also find that tennis and parties were all you had in common.) If you have less time, because of more or new work, or greater responsibilities for the children, you'll find that other friends with more time will also fall away. But consider this, something else I learned the hard way: your friends know before you do how much you have changed. You can't have gone through this searing emotional experience without it having changed you. You may be more silent, more thoughtful, less "fun" than you were, without realizing it. You may be less interested in other people's plans and lives because you have become so wrapped up in your own. Worst of all, you may have become a threat.

I'm sorry, but it's true. Singles of both sexes make couples uncomfortable. The death of a spouse reminds others of mortality, something they prefer not to think about. Divorce frightens them for other reasons. Who knows, it might be contagious. I had thought that single women were the only ones considered predatory and potentially damaging to others' marriages, but divorced and widowed men have told me that they have been warned off the premises if they spent too long talking to one man's wife. Even close couple friends cannot always find it in their hearts to keep on welcoming a "dangerous" single in their midst.

• Be prepared to make new friends. You'll have to be realistic about this. It's a whole new life you're going to be leading. The new broom is going to sweep a lot of old things out of your life. You have to be very realistic. Stop clinging to the past too tightly or you'll get stuck there.

- Stop wallowing. Don't be like that person who told me how she lay there listening to old tapes. Toss them. All those lovely memories of what a nice life you had before the fights started – forget them. Don't go back to that bar where you used to have a drink together when you were discussing your brave new plans. Don't go back to any of the places where the good times used to be. You can't go back. Nothing's there any more. Bad as things look now, it won't do you any good to remember the good old days.

- Make a list of all the bad things about your ex and all the reasons you split. When you're tempted to get dangerously sentimental, turn to paper again. Put that list on the stereo, if necessary, to remind you when you are in danger of becoming sloppily sentimental, or on the fridge door, so you won't eat your troubles away (all you'll get is fat).

- No eating, no drinking. I mean, to excess. I may have said to pour yourself a glass of wine as a ritual, but don't start *drinking*. That's no way to get over anything.

- Avoid tranquillizers. And any doctor who tries to prescribe them for you. Get a support system going that involves people, not pills. Just because you are suffering withdrawal symptoms from a person doesn't mean you should become dependent on any other addictive substances. Those withdrawal symptoms eventually could be worse.

- Don't get carried away in other people's beds (or your own). Sex is another addiction. That man who described his crazy stud behaviour realized one morning when he woke up and looked at yet another unfamiliar face that this was no way to deal with his failure. These days, of course, it's downright dangerous to fool around so much.

- Stop feeling sorry for yourself. There's a lot of pain out there; you don't have the corner on it. One of the best ways to feel better is to reach out and help someone else who is in pain. You won't have far to look.

- Count your blessings. And be grateful. If you have a child, that's the best reason to be thankful. If your parents are still living, you may find them surprisingly supportive and helpful. At times like these, you find out what families are for. And while you're at it, don't forget your ex's parents, especially if you have children. It's hard on them to lose touch with grandchildren just because the parents have split. If both sides can manage not to cast blame or hurl accusations, you may have found another source of love and support, at least for your children if not directly for yourself.

- Forgive yourself. You have to forgive your ex because you can't live with bitterness for the rest of your life; it's too damaging to you. But you also have to forgive yourself. Of course, you had a part in the failure of your marriage. There's no such thing as no-fault, despite what the new divorce laws say. But there's no reason to dwell on the faults, no matter whose they were. Look at it this way; you've learned a lot. You won't make those mistakes again. You'll make others.
- Don't shut down. Keep on being vulnerable and loving. It's the only way to survive. Trust me.

Help Is On the Way

My goodness, but there's a lot of unhappiness out there! There's also a lot of help. There are manuals and how-to books on divorce covering the range from basic instructions on the legal steps and financial considerations to emotional self-help, family counselling, and survival techniques. Like marriage, divorce is here to stay, and there's a lode of information to tap and share. Established thirty years ago, Parents Without Partners, an international organization with over 200,000 members, and chapters in most major cities in North America, was among the first support networks. There are also courses and self-help groups and counselling available across the country through churches and Ys and even in night schools and community colleges.

The first step is the hardest one.

CHAPTER NINETEEN

How to Help Your Children Survive Divorce

Tell the child that you and your husband haven't been getting along. Then get to the point slowly and carefully. — *Adrian Kulp*, fourth grade, Coopersburg, Pennsylvania

There is no doubt that divorce has a profound effect on young families. Surveys are constantly being conducted to find out how far-reaching the effect is, what kind of effect it has on children, of what age, how long the readjustment period lasts and so on. Divorce is still a huge sociological question mark, and sociologists are doing their best to find the answers. What they also have to do is assess the effect on the larger family, the one surrounding that mythical nuclear one. Relatives are affected by a divorce in the family, especially grandparents, if they are denied access to their grandchildren. The children suffer from this denial as well. Brothers and sisters of one or the other spouse often become unofficial counsellors of the injured parties (both parties are injured), and possibly role models for the affected children. We keep coming back to the children.

A divorced woman told me how happy she was, living with

her children in a shack on her parents' property, and everything was going along fine, except her kids kept bringing home
strangers for her to marry. The wife of her son's teacher died,
and the boy suggested to his mother that she marry his teacher
because the man needed a new wife and the boy a new father.
"What'll I do?" the woman asked me. You hear stories of
sabotage by kids, but you also hear stories of desperate need.

What About the Children?

In the long run, I think that divorce must be hardest on the
children. If the marriage was so untenable that it had to end,
then there is a certain amount of relief felt on the part of the
man and woman. Any relief the children may feel, especially if
they have been witnesses to terrible fights, that the battle is
over is overwhelmed by other feelings, like rejection, guilt, fear
and insecurity.

If someone left, with or without a fight, the child as well as
the abandoned parent feels rejected. The child may also feel
responsible for the departure. ("Was it something I did?") If
the child has been hustled away with the departing parent,
there are guilt feelings and worry about the other parent. The
fact that anyone left makes the child fearful about the
remaining parent. If things get too heavy, will that one leave
also? Overriding all is a terrible sense of insecurity. ("What's to
become of me?") The bottom has just dropped out of this
corner of the world. The foundations have rocked. No one
will ever be safe again.

That's the emotional view of divorce. In actual fact,
surveyors have discovered that over 50 percent of the children
of divorced parents are indistinguishable from others within
five years of the split. The most important item to guarantee
their survival is love ("love and time"). If the custodial parent is
emotionally stable (sometimes that's a big if, right after a messy
divorce) and keeps providing love and a well-structured life,
the foundation remains secure. And if the noncustodial parent
goes on assuring the child of continuing love and proves the
claim by seeing the child regularly and supporting the custodial parent, then perhaps this corner of the world will keep on

feeling safe. The second biggest problem for any child left in the custody of the mother is money. If the standard of living has gone way way down after the break-up, then of course the child is going to feel threatened, deprived and hard done by, with good reason. Life will never be the same again, nor will it ever be as good materially as it might have been, but there are compensations. Serenity within the house is one of them.

The financial deprivation shows up most clearly in the educational levels reached by students from broken homes. Another study has shown that fewer adults with high academic achievement come from one-parent homes than two-parent homes. Less education usually means lower-paying jobs, so the deprivation becomes long-term, even lifelong. It stands to reason that good schoolwork is dependent on a stable (quiet, secure) family, the guidance and attention and concern of both parents, and decent living (studying) quarters. Plus these days it costs. There's always something – a visiting play, an extra book, a school excursion – that requires money. If the kid from the divorced family doesn't have it, it hurts.

When there's too much noise, too little space, no discipline because no time to follow up on it, and bad food, a kid will go into the streets to find his space, his entertainment, the things he lacks at home. Still other surveys indicate that adolescents with single parents get into more trouble than those from two-parent families, not because of neglect in this case but because they've been on their own for too long, and they have made wrong decisions along the way about companions, behaviour, activities. Peers with similar problems apparently aren't much help. They all feel singular in their lonely, deprived state. Also resentful.

How to Tell if Your Child Needs Help

It shows in the schoolwork first. If your child or adolescent has stopped concentrating, stopped doing homework, started getting more detentions and worsening grades, there's trouble brewing. Sometimes, when they can't keep up, or when they can't afford to do what everyone else seems to be able to do (the class excursion, play, etc.), they get defiant first, then aggressive. They adopt a what-do-I-care attitude and try to bluff their way out of their humiliation. They become anti-social so they won't have to admit to their peers that they have problems. Others may become anti-social in another way – hiding in their books and refusing to take part in any group activities. Schoolwork then becomes an escape from reality.

As if you didn't have enough to worry about. But you don't stop being a parent when you stop being a spouse. You're responsible for more than the physical well-being of your children; you have to look after their emotional and psychological needs as well. Fortunately, it's not really that hard. What it takes (you may have heard this before) is love and time. You may not have much money, and heaven knows, you're pressed for time, but you should be able to supply the love. It's the emotional stability that is most necessary to assure the child that all is still right with this small world. What matters most is love.

How to Nurture
The magic word is nurturance. People need nurturing, not only small people but big people as well. Women traditionally have been the nurturers, but men (some men) are slowly learning how to nurture. Here's a list of what it takes to nurture:

- Showing affection, both verbally and physically.
- Building trust, including a respect for each child's privacy.
- Doing things together – the sooner you start this the better, and then you'll find you have the time (this includes eating together – see dinner, page 125 – holidays, outings and so on).
- Developing support systems within the family (this requires loyalty and commitment), including relatives outside the immediate family unit.

Communication and Emotional Health

Communication, of course, is vital to nurturance. (If you think I'm repeating myself, I am; see communication, page 111.) Communication is vital to emotional health, and if there's anyone who needs to be emotionally healthy, it's you and your kids at a time like this. (Read as well Sven Wahlroos's *Family Communication*.)

Here are some qualities of emotional health, all based on communication, that are especially important to encourage in kids after a divorce:

- The ability to help yourself and others. What we don't realize is that doing is a form of communication. For some inarticulate people, it's the only way they communicate. See what they do, don't wait to hear what they're not saying.
- Freedom of choice. When one has no choice, there is no communication. If children have to toe the party line, they're not going to be very open about any rebellious feelings they may have.
- Inner security. When children have self-esteem, they will have the confidence to take risks with other people, to reach out, to form relationships.
- The ability to postpone needs. The ability to postpone immediate gratification is one of the real signs of maturity. The ability to communicate one's needs without demanding their immediate fulfillment is a communication skill beyond many adults, but it's a sure sign of emotional health.
- Being able to evaluate emotional reality. One kid commented to his mother that he could tell when she'd had a bad day without her having to tell him. Families know each other. If they're allowed to be honest, they can communicate their feelings, and tolerate them, too, without too many words actually being said.
- Deep and lasting relationships. The ability to form lasting relationships again is based on the fine skills of communication, which in turn require all the foregoing qualities: trust, security, self-esteem and so on.
- The ability to learn from experience. After a divorce both parents and children learn from sad experience, and if they

can share what they've learned, all can grow. Perhaps this is where a divorced or bereaved family has an advantage over the intact one, though it's a hard-won benefit and not one I'd wish on anyone.

- Enthusiasm. Being able to share enthusiasm sounds easy, but lots of people can't share their joys any more readily than they can share their heartaches. As with other such communication, it takes two to do it – the giver of news and the receiver. Both must be enthusiastic and also sincere.

- The ability to identify with others. Knowing and expecting that others care what happens to you as you care what happens to them is the beginning of humanitarianism and leads to a certain knowledge about society – that we are all, in fact, our brother's and sister's keepers.

- Faith. No matter what you choose to call it, faith is essential to basic communication. In its lowest form, it is a recognition that everyone counts, that we all deserve to breathe the same air, that what each individual does is important to all of humanity.

Therefore, you give your children the time of day. With that, and love, they may survive your divorce.

CHAPTER TWENTY

Custody

When I can no longer bear to think of the victims of broken homes, I begin to think of the victims of intact ones. — *Peter de Vries*

The one (sadly) reassuring fact about a death in the family is that when it's over, it's over. The surviving spouse gets to keep all the forks and the stereo; the kids know whom they have to turn to. With divorce, on the other hand, the complications are just beginning. After the division of spoils comes the division of the children. It's hell for parents, and it sure isn't easy on a kid. Oddly enough, the children of bereaved homes are more likely to have problems at school, especially boys, especially if the female parent died. (I'm not just telling you what I read; I've observed this one.)

The Custody Battle In Bertolt Brecht's play *The Good Woman of Setzuan*, a judge has to decide which mother keeps a child of contention: the woman who physically bore him or the one who saved him from death and took care of him. The judge (you may begin to recognize the story) orders each mother to take an arm of the child and pull. The one who wins this human tug-of-war will win the child. The biological mother won't let go; the other one relinquishes her hold rather than hurt the child. The judge awards the child to her. Judges still play God. The child is still the one who stands to be the most damaged by the split in the family that led to this tug-of-war.

This isn't what either of you had in mind at all. When that precious scrap of humanity was born, that baby was a miracle, and one that you vowed you would keep safe from tigers. Babies bring out the best in fathers and mothers. All the parents' care and tenderness, even ignorant care and uninformed tenderness, is focussed on this little link of their union and this fragile hope of the future. And now – this isn't what you had in mind at all – you are warring and bitter, and the children often become weapons you use to hurt each other.

Not that parents intend to use a child as a weapon, not at first. They want only what is best for the children; they intend to reach some agreement that is least disruptive to the family. Hah. Then someone starts apportioning the money and the time, and then somehow the love is in short supply, too.

The reason there are so many female lone parents is that they get custody of the children. The reason they get custody is that fathers have seldom contested it, until recently. When fathers do contest, they get custody in 74 percent of cases. The good women of Setzuan often give up the child because of the material advantages to be gained – for the child. When mothers are awarded custody and support payments, in 90 percent of those cases the support payments are defaulted. Fathers leave town, leave the province, start new families and forget their first family.

That's one scenario, too cynical, I know, but also too frequent. There's another side to it, also bitter. When the mother has the child for all but two weeks twice a year, or every other weekend, she has the opportunity to tell her side of the story, a very one-sided side. All the rankling injustice, all the cruelties and neglect, the continuing short-changing and wrangling are recounted to the child, dropped like poison in the ears. It's a wise child who knows his own father, the saying goes, and it was never truer than in a lopsided custody case. This is why some men finally give up. They leave, physically and emotionally, because it's a no-win situation. They have lost their children; their children have been lost to them; they go away to try again. I don't have to tell you the horror stories of pain on both sides, of cruelties both petty and heinous, all leading to an erosion of trust and love that cannot be restored. We've all listened to the tales that divorced parents tell.

But What About the Children?

In spite of that report that says that 50 percent of children of divorce are indistinguishable from children of intact families five years down the line, that still leaves 50 percent who aren't. The qualifying factors that enable some to be relatively unscathed are difficult to guarantee: a stable environment in a family that just became unstable; security when it just became dependent on a meagre, precarious child payment; emotional support when one prop is absent and the present one still angry. Not great.

And so, little by little, the courts have come around to the idea of joint custody, equal apportioning of time and responsibility. There has been a growing recognition of the value to the child of a joint custodial arrangement and even, more recently, of a "presumption" in its favour. It's a fashion whose time has come. Is it a good one?

The Legal Aspects

When exclusive custody is legally awarded to one parent, with access rights to the other, the latter is virtually excluded from the child's life. He (in the past more usually he) becomes a visitor, never knowing what's going on, buying favours with no guarantee of love. On the other hand, the mother feels she's the ogre, the one who has to make the rules and enforce them daily, the one who has to skimp and save and serve the daily portion of denial and discipline. Daddy becomes Big Daddy, heavy-handed with the goodies and far too lenient because, what the hell, it's holiday time and he only sees the kid twice a year or every other weekend or whatever. If he left, he may also be spending conscience money to make up for what he did. Theoretically, he is supposed to continue to exercise some parental authority and to have some say about the child's education, but too often a summit conference with the other parent ends in war, so what's the use?

So joint custody is handed down to avoid this feeling on the part of one parent of being left out and to encourage the maintenance (illusion?) of co-parenting. Originally, joint custody did not include physical custody or the daily care and control of the child; this was awarded to one parent, with access rights given to the other. Obviously, that has changed now. Most cases of joint custody involve the physical co-parenting as well as legal decisions concerning the child. The daily responsibility is shared between the two parents.

Two Stories

I personally know of two cases of joint custody. In one, the parents live just streets apart, so the children can divide their time week by week and go to the same school no matter where they have breakfast. The kids give their schedules to their friends so they can be found. In the other case, one of a preschool child, the parents also share her week by week. They live in the same city but too far apart for one school to accommodate their addresses. Later on, they'll have to find a special school, or one of them will have to move. In both cases, the parents have not remarried.

I know many other cases where the father has remarried and his children by his first wife come weekends. There are lots of complications here. Some relate to the stepmother (see steps, page 181), others to her children by a former marriage, and additional ones to the children of the new family. Money is often a problem, as well as the fair apportioning thereof.

Is joint custody the answer? I suppose it depends on the question.

In the Child's Interests

In the best of all possible worlds, the loving presence of both parents in a child's life is the way things should be. Socially, materially and emotionally, the child is better off when centred in the family of origin. Well, we all know that, don't we? Now, how do we go about doing the least damage possible, given all the other damaging factors? The one thing any parent surely wants to avoid is to turn the child into a football being kicked back and forth by these ex-teammates trying to score points for themselves.

If joint custody is going to become another form of competition, then certainly it's not in the best interests of the child. Alternating week by week can be confusing, even if the parents are neighbours (physically, that is). Keeping track of one's underwear and favourite toys in two different homes, let alone the busy schedules of two disparate parents, requires corporate efficiency from a kid who hasn't learned long division yet. The really frightening aspect of such an arrangement is that the children can't help thinking that their parents will get back together again. An illusion of normality and friendly co-operation can set up false hopes. On the other hand, on-again off-again weekends, with hot and cold running parents, are also not good. In the short term, the competition may seem to serve the child's best acquisitive interests, but in the longer term the children know they're being wooed to hand out favours.

Woman's Point of View

When the mother is the chief custodial parent, she is usually forced into seriously straitened circumstances since there's simply not enough money. She probably tries to work outside the home as well (for inadequate pay) and to run a household single-handed. She suffers from overwork, frustration, isolation and anxiety. Trying to make all the decisions herself, she actually creates family tensions. She has no time for a social life. As for a second marriage, who's going to take her on with all those kids?

Oddly enough, though joint custody sounds fair, this too can hurt the mother financially. No support payments are ordered. The thinking is that since the two parents will alternate physical support, each will have a similar financial burden to carry: food, shelter, clothes, medical costs and so on. Many fathers actually profit financially by joint custody orders, while mothers lose out. Even if the woman works to pay for her side of her commitments, women still only get paid 60 to

64 percent of what men earn, so she is hard-pressed to meet her share of the obligations. This is another consideration. A woman must take a close look at the joint physical custody order and ensure that there is a fair division of the financial responsibilities for the children's support, and some hope of her own survival.

Man's Point of View

One of the main reasons men cop out of support payments is that they get terribly frustrated trying to be a parent when they can't get at the kids. They have lost the currency of the daily exchange, so they can't contribute meaningfully to their children's lives. Their exes are denying them real knowledge of what's going on, hampering their efforts to maintain a normal relationship with the kids and dropping poison about them into the little one's ears. Is it any wonder they give up and go off and start a second family they can call their own?

So is joint custody the answer to keep a father in touch with his children? A lot of fathers are not that organized when it comes to arranging their kids' lives. Sharing custody can often mean more work than they ever did before. Studies show that the mother in a joint custody situation will usually do more than her share when it comes to shopping for the kids' clothes, making and keeping their doctors' appointments, planning their excursions and holidays, and so on. When she doesn't do it, it's the children who suffer, and complain, and the father who accuses her of not co-operating. More often than not, the father solves his side of the problem by turning to a relative, a nanny or a new wife to do the work for him. (I really am trying to be unbiased about this, but I am reporting facts.)

Fathers are perfectly capable of taking full responsibility for their children, and I know many (younger) fathers who can and do. All it takes is experience, and all experience takes is practise. Part of the trouble is in the way that (older) men have been raised, with no expectation of this kind of responsibility. And whose fault is that? That's why it is so important for men to share in the nurturance a family provides. Then, in the sad event of a split in their families of procreation, they will be able to provide their children with the support and care they need.

What Children Need After a Divorce in the Family

You can't go back. You can't knit up all the unravelled threads of a marital relationship. What you have to do is concentrate on the present and try to make it as serene and comprehensible as you can to your children. Here are a few things you can give them:

- Maintenance of meaningful relationships with both parents.
- Predictability in the living arrangements.
- Stability – same school, same friends, same lifestyle, if possible.
- That means, then, adequate financial support.
- Assurance that both parents will continue to love them.
- Reassurance that it's not their fault, not something they did.
- Trust – that both parents will continue to be there for them and be honest with them.
- A promise of the future in terms of educational plans, preparation for life.
- Security – not financial security but a firm assurance of their worth to the family (and ultimately to society).
- Self-esteem.

These are things that any child needs, whether the product of a broken home or not.

CHAPTER TWENTY-ONE

How to Cope as a Single Parent

No one can yet gauge the subterranean impact of a generation of single parenthood on the lives of children. — *Newsweek*

An oxymoron is "a figure of speech in which contradictory words or connotations are placed together." Example: lead balloon, hurry slowly. If ever there was an oxymoron, it's the single parent. Only it's not a figure of speech. This is real life. Very real.

Single parents are not a new phenomenon, but they're more visible, they're poorer, and the reasons for their single-ness are different from those in the past. In the past, lone-parent families tended to disappear. Widowed women went back to their families of origin and raised their children with the support of their family and community. Widowers with children usually remarried, more often than the widows, but there were more of them then.

Although the present-day causes that leave parents single are more frequently divorce or separation rather than child-birth mortality or war, about one-third of lone parents are still bereaved. There is one other category of single parent: the ones rearing children outside of wedlock, an increasing situation today as young unwed mothers choose to keep their babies rather than give them up for adoption and as older single women choose parenthood without marriage.

In any case, these families do not today return to their families of origin; sometimes it's too far to go, sometimes they aren't there any more. Whether from need or choice, they try to remain independent, raising their children on (minuscule) widows' and orphans' allowances or (grudged, defaulted) support payments, (skimpy, humiliating) welfare or mothers' allowance cheques, or whatever kind of (low-paying) work they can get that will still enable them to keep a home for their children. Two-thirds of all single parents live below the poverty line, and most of those are women. They are probably among the most stressed parents in our society today, and their children the most economically and socially disadvantaged. The majority of lone parents, as I say, are mothers. The picture we get of them is another aspect of the feminization of poverty.

Housing

Both male and female lone parents suffer the poorest housing conditions. At the bottom end of the wage scale, housing costs disproportionately more of the family dollar, from 30 to 50 percent of total income. As I was working on this section I heard someone on the radio reporting that frequently 75 percent of the (welfare) income is going for shelter now. That doesn't leave much for food, clothing, medical care, education, or anything else the family's heart desires, let alone needs.

Surveys turn up some strange figures and discoveries. It has been found that in a comparison of the living arrangements of male and female lone-parent families, the women were much more likely to be living without additional persons (other than their children) than their male counterparts were. In other words, the males are shacked up with someone, probably of the female persuasion.

Several years ago, when I was investigating the living conditions of an old age pensioner by living on the Old Age Pension myself, I used to go to a women's hostel for Sunday dinner (guaranteed vegetables and conversation). I asked the advice of an acquaintance I had made there, a woman living on welfare. I was being pursued by a man in the rooming house I was in and wanted to know what to to about it. Her reply: "Just don't live common-law, or they'll take away your welfare!"

Apart from that deterrent – that is, the spectre of losing one's income, however meagre, if one had a live-in friend of the opposite sex – a female lone parent is not likely to find someone willing to take on her and her children *and* her poverty. That's why 75 percent of single mothers are "maintainers," according to the Census – that is, living without other adult persons in their households. Aside from the fact that there's no one to share or help out with the expenses, there's also no one to help out with anything – with the kids, with the work, with the reassurance and support and relentlessness of it all. It's lonely.

The Good News?

Surveys turn up odd facts. A single working mother with two children does less housework than a married working woman with one child and one husband. Reason: the kids help the single mother; the husband doesn't help his wife much. I have always maintained that husbands were very time-consuming, but there are other reasons to have them around. For one thing, they do go to the drug store at night to get more cough syrup. For another thing, they're good for the morale. They may not get up in the night with a sick child, but they make nice comforting noises and worry about it with you, if they're awake. (The only time I ever got mad at my husband was when he was asleep and I wished I were.) That emotional support is important.

One of the dangers of being a single parent is that one tends to lean on the kids too much, both for companionship (not bad) and for emotional support (not good). It's nice for kids to have the single parent's undivided attention, which they are more likely to have in the absence of the other parent.

But the parent cannot expect the children to fill in the gaps left by the missing spouse. Women, particularly, tend to relate more to their daughters and to treat them like dormitory pals. That's fine, up to a point, but it can be hard on the child. Don't burden her with too many secrets and don't expect her to help you make your weighty decisions.

Information about how female lone parents relate to their sons, particularly over the age of sixteen, was not considered until lately. Now, wouldn't you know, there's been a book published about it (Linda Forcey, *Mothers and Sons: Toward an Understanding of Responsibility*). Forcey thinks that as women have developed their own strengths, they're getting better at handling their sons, and they have some joyous stories to tell. (I could have told her a few.) The one danger I have observed of single mothers' relationships with their sons is that of leaning too hard. In fact, you have to be careful with both sexes. Don't press the girl-child into becoming "mommy's little helper" or the boy-child into becoming the "man of the house" now that Daddy's gone. It's more pressure than either can or should bear. I call it emotional blackmail. You're still the grown-up. Keep it that way.

A Word for Single Fathers
The single parents who are having a hard time these days are the fathers. They're often victimized by sex stereotypes and don't get the support that women do. Much more isolated because more rare, they don't get any breaks, financial or emotional. Parenthood and nurturing are not magical attributes that belong only to women. In fact, as more men learn to nurture, they're going to change the world. As St. Augustine said, "Give me other mothers and I will give you another world." Fathers can be mothers, too.

Tranquil Homes Are Best
If only we could be paid for anxiety, by the hour, we'd be laughing – and then we wouldn't get paid any more. We worry so much about our children: their health, their welfare, their

happiness, their future. We are constantly second-guessing, questioning, berating ourselves: if only we hadn't done this, if only things had turned out differently, if only whatever. You can't live with if-onlies. That way lies madness. Let's try and think of a few positive things, even for poor, lonely, frightened, overworked, anxious, single parents.

- Anything is better for your kids than the battles they were witnessing and suffering from in the former marriage.
- You're a nice person now, even if you're harassed and overworked.
- You can give your child more close attention because there isn't an adult competing for it.
- Raising a child at the best of times is an adventure. Doing it alone is a major achievement.
- Children are still the source of the most gratuitous pleasure there is. Enjoy it/them.
- Chickens come from broken homes, and they do all right. (Old saying.)
- Tranquil homes are best.

Now, if we could just stop teachers from going overboard on Mother's Day and Father's Day, single parents could be almost reconciled to their lot.

PART FIVE

Remarriage

CHAPTER TWENTY-TWO

How to Succeed the Second Time Around

A wife lasts only for the length of the marriage, but an ex-wife is there for the rest of your life. — Jim Samuels

Anyone entering a second marriage with the expectation that it will be like the first one is nuts (that's a technical term, meaning naive, unrealistic, overly optimistic and nuts). Even more second marriages fail than first ones – 44 percent of them – and the main reason is trouble with the children from the first marriage(s). The new mate tries to be a parent to the other spouse's children. Big mistake.

Poor second wife! We have all inherited a number of negative cultural stereotypes about her. She is the Other Woman and the Wicked Stepmother. On the other hand, stepfathers are now getting the rap for the majority of child abuse. For heaven's sake, let's be careful before we start generalizing. Having issued that warning, I am going to start generalizing.

Second Wife
A second wife polarizes the feelings of the first wife and the

children. A first wife will often focus all her resentment and anger on the second wife and try to get even with her ex through the other woman (though she may not have been "the other woman"). This is where the horror stories about money begin, with more demands for support, suits for back support payments, garnisheeing of wages, attempts to bring the second couple's standard of living down to or below the first family's. One second wife took over her husband's two children by his first wife and cared for them in her home for eight years, only to have the first wife sue for eight years' child support at the end of that time. Nothing was in writing but the original legal agreement, so the husband had to pay up, and there was no recompense for the second wife's services. This is part of the other side of the sad story of the impoverished and abandoned – and very bitter – single parent.

As for the children of the first marriage, their jealousy and insecurity are also directed at the second wife. Although she may well not be the reason her husband left his first wife, she is the living proof that he will never reconcile the differences that split the first marriage. She is the tangible threat to any promise the father ever made to their mother and – who knows? – to them. He says he will love them forever, but he said that to Mother, too, and look what happened to that promise.

Reconstituted Families

I love the term *reconstituted*. It makes me think of orange juice. Well, if it's general advice you want about how to reconstitute a marriage, here's a list of recommendations compiled from a number of sources over the past couple of years.

The Blended Marriage!
From frozen concentrate:
Just add TLC and stir.

- Make sure you know the difference between history and ghosts: appreciate the past without walking backward into the sunset.

- Keep some keepsakes but don't overdo. A museum of artifacts from anyone's Other Life requires a lot of dusting.
- If you can, don't live in either house of the previous marriages. Start your own home.
- For the same obvious reason, try to buy some new furniture common to both of you. Would it be tactless of me to suggest you don't sleep in either previous conjugal bed?
- Marry a friend. (See friends, page 197.) You should know that by now.
- Marry someone you love. That may seem obvious, but there's such a thing as rebound. Marriage is still called "for better or for worse" and you want to make this one better, so be sure.
- Trust – it's the beginning and the reason for fidelity.
- Change your expectations: no one can be all things to someone else. You found that out already. Be realistic this time, both of you.
- You should be very clear about money. (See money, page 39.) It's even more complicated the second time around.
- In fact, it would be a good idea, this time around, to draw up a marriage contract.
- What about the kids? No one can legislate love, but at least get the logistics straight about visiting, custody, finances and – is it too much to hope for? – discipline.
- Sex. By this time you know what turns you on, don't you? Let's hope you both do. No surprises (well, some, of course), but make sure you agree on what's a surprise and what's a shock.
- Are you *sure* this isn't rebound?

What you need, as always, is a commitment – to your spouse, to your marriage, to your love.

Subliminal Emotions

Second wives, I'm afraid, are not without their own little arsenal of weapons and reasons to use them. A second wife tends to feel fiercely protective of her new husband and of their new life together. She is not above trying to sabotage the first wife, the support payments (that she feels she is helping to pay for now), the expectations of help. She wouldn't be human if she didn't feel some pangs of jealousy over the past when her husband was happy being part of another family. What she has to remember is that was then, this is now. So here are a few rules that might be helpful for a second wife to keep in mind. Note: they apply to second husbands, too:

- Don't forget your self-esteem and your autonomy.
- Always be grateful for the past. It made you and your mate what you are today. You wouldn't be here if things hadn't turned out the way they did.
- If you still find it difficult to accept the other's history, it might help you to write it down, not exhaustively, not a complete biography, just the highlights as you discover them. You can keep a little private file and add to it as you gather new insights. Don't dig for information; let it come up naturally. But write it down and take a look at it once in a while. It may help you to understand your mate better.
- Move on. Start creating your own new history.
- You can afford not to be jealous, so don't be.
- Let go. Stop harbouring old resentments, past quarrels. Wipe the slate clean.
- Stay out of it. Stay out of any court proceedings your ex is still having with the first spouse.
- Don't compete.
- Forgive. I've said this before in another context, but it bears repeating. Forgive the first mate if he or she is causing trouble. Forgive the children and try to understand how frightened and betrayed they feel. Forgive yourself if you've been less than generous or kind. You're all human, just trying to muzzy along as best you can.
- It wouldn't hurt to laugh – at yourself, with others.

CHAPTER TWENTY-THREE

How to Be a Step

Yard sale: Recently married couple is combining households. All duplicates will be sold, except children. — *Classified ad*

Maybe it *would* be easier if you could sell the children – not easier for the kids but for the couple. Second marriages are nothing like firsts, and it's mainly because of the kids. You certainly can't blame them: look what they've lost, through no fault of their own. When a new parent (a step, male or female) comes into the family picture on either side, there has to be trouble. Are you sure you want to go through with this?

Talk It Over

You've met someone and you are seriously contemplating remarriage, but you're understandably nervous about it. This time you want it to take. You're sure about your new mate, but can you handle the residuals – the children from the previous marriage? If you're going to be a step and are nervous about it, it might be wise to go to a counsellor before you marry. Go together with your potential mate and go separately. Try to identify problem areas before they arise. Spell out your expectations. Most people wait until trouble starts before they seek help, the theory being why fix something if it isn't broken. But something *was* broken – a former marriage. You don't want it to happen again. Some people can work things out without professional assistance. If you and your future spouse take the time to sit down and talk to each other as freely as you would before a counsellor, you may be able to do it yourself.

How to Get in Training

There are other things you can do to get in training as a step. (If you already are one, go back and cover what you missed. Some of them, obviously, can't be done after the fact; the opportunity for others only arises with time.)

- Have a few dry runs with all members of the family involved, say some trial outings, weekends, whatever. Start with food or outside entertainment so you can be distracted and won't notice awkward silences when they fall. Eric Berne (*Games People Play*) identifies different ways of relating to people, some meaningful and some not. Pastimes are not meaningful, but they are pleasant and they give you a chance to get to know each other in a nonthreatening way. They also begin to give you a new history of your own: New Family Outings I Have Known.

- At the same time, there's such a thing as too much of a good thing. The Good Times are not always the best preparation for reality. Have some ordinary times, too, so the stepkids can see that you're for real, knobs and all.

- But don't let anyone pin knobs on you that you don't have. If you get the idea (and you will) that you are being cast as the Other Woman/Man when in truth you met your mate three years after the divorce, then get that out in the open and get it straight. You'll have all the heavies laid on that you can manage without a blatant piece of miscasting.

- Don't make unrealistic plans. If you've never been a cookie-baking type, don't start now. You're not going to be Superstep.

- Listen. (See listening, page 113.) When you progress to quieter times with the children, take time to listen. Listen creatively, contribute, exchange, but mainly listen. Find out what's behind the belligerence (fear), the silence (resentment), the rudeness (anger), whatever. At the same time, don't force the relationship. You may be listening to a lot of silence at first. I never said this was going to be easy. Just try to remember who's grown-up.

- Remember that, and know yourself. You have to know your fears, too, and your limitations. As the grammatical worm said when she turned, "There are some things up with which I will not put!" You're going to have to make those things clear.
- Don't say no – at least not for quite a while. Try not to put yourself into the position of witch or ogre. That's not to say you have to be a doormat, but watch it.
- House rules maybe should be posted, or at least spelled out. Make them few and make them simple, but make them clear. (See rules, page 55.) This will be your home, and you want your stepchildren to feel at home in it, but never quite as at home as at home because it isn't. You live here.
- Keep your self-respect. That's why the rules; that's why you'll be nice but not wimpy.
- But don't stop being nice. You have to keep reassuring these kids that you are not the wicked stepmother. Be helpful. Be available. Praise them – when there's something to praise them about. Be genuine. Be, above all, trustworthy. If there's one thing stepchildren need, it's adults they can trust. Well, all children need that, but all children don't have the reason to doubt that these do.
- Talk to your mate. It's called communication. Find out what he or she expects of you in relation to the children. How much are you expected to be involved? (Be warned: circumstances change. Often one of the first things a first wife will do is give up custody now that the children have a whole home to go to and she can try to patch up her life.)
- Don't interfere, and also don't offer unnecessary comments, odious comparisons, or snide I-told-you-so's. Your mate will ask your advice about the kids when it's wanted. Be a sympathetic sounding board, but stay out of the family fights. If you say something you'll regret, you'll regret it. They'll forgive each other, but they won't forgive you. If you have children of your own, you'll understand that without being told.
- Steps who have children of their own often bend over backward not to play favourites. But that shouldn't stop you from protecting your children and for standing up for them

when you feel they're right. You can't help it if you love them best. They're your flesh and blood. Remembering that may help you understand why the Others feel as they do.

- Hope for friendship. Love is an unsolicited gift.

The Witch Syndrome

Stepmothers in the past have had very bad press. Snow White could tell you a story about her stepmother that would make you choke. Hansel's and Gretel's stepmother browbeat her husband into abandoning those darling children who did nothing to her but eat. Stepmothers get it from both parties – the wife and the children of the first marriage. Ms. C will tell you more than you care to hear about her mean old stepmother and miserable stepsisters who left her to sit in the ashes while they sashayed off to that ball. Because stepmothers have been in a no-win situation, today they tend to overcompensate. They try too hard to succeed with their stepchildren, and they and their marriages fail.

Why is it usually the woman? Answer: because more divorced men remarry, and because divorced men in Canada tend to choose younger, never-married, childless women as their second wives. (Stepfathers have their problems, too, and we'll get to them.) So more women get to be stepmothers, and, by corollary, wicked witches. They never meant to be witches. They don't feel like witches. What they feel like is a combination of punching bag and victim. They're everyone's favourite target.

Steps After Death

In Ms. C's time, mothers died in childbirth. That's why there are so many stepmothers in fairy tales. The poor, distraught widowers married again because they simply couldn't manage the little babies they were left with. They usually married widows, like Ms. C's stepmother, and then if they died themselves, as Ms. C's father did, well, that left the orphaned child in a terrible bind. That doesn't happen often nowadays, although I can think of two cases where it did. In both, the child, a boy, and teenaged by the time his last natural parent died, left home.

Death used to create stepfamilies; now divorce is the prerequisite. Surveys indicate that the happiest second marriages are those between two bereaved people, presumably because there are no living exes lying about, but more likely because each person usually emerged saddened but serene from a happy, successful marriage and has full expectation of the same again. But (another survey) it's even harder to be a stepparent after death than after divorce. Why? Because:

- When a parent remarries after the death of the other parent, even adult children resent it. The children are usually adult (but perhaps not mature) because on average divorce hits people earlier than death. Again because of the age element, there are probably fewer children involved in a second marriage after divorce than after death.
- A mourning parent was a comforting memorial. The dead parent could be idealized. By remarrying, the living parent just removed the pedestal.
- The longer a bereaved spouse takes to remarry, the more the children don't want a new one. They're used to the way things were. This is true of children of divorced parents, too.
- Children of a dead parent often live with the surviving one. If the remarriage creates a home in which they don't feel welcome, or if they can't stand their parent's new spouse, they have no place to go but out.

A Few Rueful Statistics

Wives used to die, as I said, in childbirth. As late as the beginning of this century, the life expectancy of a woman was only 48 years, because of childbirth mortality. Now it's 78.5 years, and counting. More commonly now the man dies first, leaving the woman to carry on alone, with miles to go before she sleeps. The average age at which a woman is widowed in North America is 56; fewer than one in ten widows remarry. So a widow's children are relatively safe from steps. Not so the children of divorced parents. The rate of remarriage among divorced (and widowed) men is now higher than the first-time marriage rate.

Enter the Stepmother

The stepmother is the eternal outsider, never able to be part of the history of the first family and therefore not allowed to understand it or share it; never real mother in terms of privileges or respect though often required to perform the services of Mother the Drone; not quite maiden aunt (if she were she wouldn't be sleeping with Dad) but sometimes as innocent and clueless as maiden aunts are supposed to be; a spurious, make-believe sister because sometimes closer in age to her stepdaughters than to her husband, but she sleeps with the beloved enemy. She thinks if she is nice and helpful that she can at least be of some use. She is in danger of being used and abused. And she has about her new family feelings as ambivalent as theirs about her. Oh, life is fraught! It's also unfair. But whoever said it wasn't?

To tell the truth, the children aren't the only ones who are overcome with waves of hostility. Steps are human, too, and can take only so much abuse before they turn and lash out. If you have done so, then you feel guilty. But you can't pretend to love these monsters. Who *could* love these monsters? They are aliens; your mate's first spouse must have come from a horrible alien planet. And they think you're weird.

Each party involved suspects the other of snooping. The first spouse, you're sure, pumps the children and wants to know everything that goes on in your house. (You, on the other hand, want to know what went on in Life Before You.) You never get any privacy, nothing is sacred, it's not just the space – never meant to accommodate all these bodies, even if it's only weekends – it's also the mind-time. You married again because you wanted to be with this person always and forever (this time), and look what's happened. You never see each other, not in private, not with any decent time. And don't talk about sex! Didn't anyone ever tell those kids that when a door is shut that means you want some privacy?

Weekend Parenting

In normal (that is, once only) marriages, the couple has a fighting chance of doing something together on weekends, albeit sandwiched among the errands, shopping, home renovations and laundry. But in a second marriage to someone who only gets to see the children on (maybe every other?) weekend, then it's party-time, play-time, special-treat-time (read expensive time) with the kids. You can't blame the weekend parent, but you get a very clear picture of your relative importance in the scheme of things, don't you? And romance? Forget it! You may be too exhausted to notice, anyway, after ten laps around the zoo, a swimming party and a barbecue.

Here are a few hints weekend parents have given me to bear in mind:

- Whatever the details of your visitation agreements, adhere to them carefully. Don't annoy the other spouse by being careless about times or dates. There might be repercussions.
- Frequent, scheduled visits are best, so the kids aren't too strange. It's hard on a parent (usually the father) to feel so remote from his children's lives. As the step, whether male or female, have some sympathy for your new spouse's feelings, torn as they probably are.
- No surprises, especially last-minute ones. Don't change the time or pick-up place; don't be late or early; return the child at the agreed-upon time. If you make special plans that require different clothes or equipment, let the kids know well in advance.
- Don't ever bargain about visitation rights or use them as a club to gain other advantages. You're bargaining with children's feelings (and lives). No wonder they may resent the step if they think they've been pushed around.
- Kids can cope with complicated living and custody arrangements, but not with unpredictability. Be the same with them. Let them know they can trust you. This goes for all parents, step and biological.
- They may even get to like the juggling act. Don't let them take unfair advantage of your guilt feelings.

Things Stepkids Say

While we're trying to condense your problems to twenty-five words or less (the solutions take longer), let's consider, too, some typical things stepchildren say that really let you know what you're facing:

- "You're not my Mommy/Daddy." (That's the basic problem right there.)
- "Mommy cooks this better than you," or "Mommy doesn't make me eat (fill in the blank)," or "Mom lets me do that (whatever it is you forbid)," or "That isn't the way Mom does that."
- "My Dad lets me watch television," or "My Dad ties shoelaces (or whatever) better than that," or "I want to talk to my Dad," or "I'll ask/tell/complain to my Dad."
- "When are you leaving?"

Listen to the Other Messages

If you can be detached enough to hear all that and to listen to the pain and uncertainty, the desperate need for something comfortable and familiar to latch onto, the inverted pride, the suppressed fear and the total helplessness of the speaker, then you deserve the Step of the Year Award. Stepchildren are pretty desolate. Their world was already disrupted once, when their parents split (or one died). Now it's upheaval time again, with another "parent" thrust upon them. They've never been given any choice (nor should they be – that way lies other horrors. I mean, it's your life), and they feel powerless in the face of a hidden agenda. But stepparents have to be saints to put up with some stepchildren's efforts to retaliate. And marriages have been known to fail because of the stepparent's inability to cope. It's a serious matter.

Assistance for Steps

Stepmothers of the past had help. The Wicked Queen had a cookbook with a recipe for apples that would knock you out; Cinderella's stepmom had a will of iron and two sneaky daughters who made life miserable for the kid (this still goes on). These days, we have professional counsellors. If all else fails, go to one.

As with other problems, however, a sense of humour can carry you over a lot of awkwardness and anger. So can paper. Try writing down your problems, hopes, frustrations. You may find out what you really think. Take it one step further. Read what you have written to your partner. When it's on paper it's possible to state your problems without raising your voice; you simply read them out, as calmly as possible. Putting things on paper gives you an agenda to work from. You will find, as I have, that paper is your best friend. (And it's cheaper than a shrink.)

Money Again

Speaking of which, I do have to say a word about the financial problems of second marriages. I talked a little about marriage contracts and family law (see family law, page 148) when I considered divorce, but remarriage creates new financial strain, especially if there are child support payments to meet. Second wives often find themselves working to pay for the first wife's children and understandably feel resentful. Still, children's needs must be met; they're their father's children, too. Provinces are putting teeth into legislation regarding child support payments with provisions for garnisheeing the father's wages even if he has left the province where his children live. There's no way around it.

If the second marriage produces children as well, finances may be especially strained. Both partners must be very open and clear about their responsibilities and attitudes and must agree about the dispersal of their assets. A marriage contract is essential, and so are wills. Be sure to revise them, and update your insurance and other contracts. Under the new divorce laws, a first wife is entitled to a share of her ex-husband's pension plan. Be sure to get it all spelled out and clear before you make any plans of your own. Property assets, too, must be considered carefully. In the case of a house owned by one or the other of the new partners (more common among second marriages), agree in advance and in writing about its division in the case of death or (perish the thought) divorce.

In another book, Lynne MacFarlane and I advised wives to be sure they own their husband's insurance policy so that he could not change the beneficiary in the event of a divorce and remarriage. If you're a second wife, you may not think much of that idea, but I can't be inconsistent. I still say it. Both the first family and the remarriage family have to learn to balance and be reconciled to all the ties that still bind them. Be civil.

PART SIX

Marriage in the Almost Twenty-First Century

CHAPTER TWENTY-FOUR

How to Maintain Intimacy

Sex is one of the nicest games there is and it's even nicer when it's played between very close friends, like husband and wife. — *Betty Jane Wylie*

What Is Sex For?

Well, of course, sex is to express love and lust. Yes, but what else is sex for? Outside marriage, it's for kicks, it's for challenge, it's for some reassurance, it's for give-a-little and get-a-little, and, of course, it's for pleasure. It's a game, a pastime, a pursuit.

Sex within marriage has a lot more variations and satisfactions than sex without. I can say that because I've looked at sex from both sides now (and you're free to argue that I really don't know sex at all). Outside marriage (or a long-term relationship) sex is like dinner out. It's an event, an occasion, something you prepare for, order and arrange carefully, savour during, linger over, remember after. This is all great. But what if you just want a hot dog? Or milk toast?

Sex within marriage is so much more than dinner out. Sex in marriage is, sure, for coloured lights and making the earth move. It's also for comfort, nurture, release, fun and quick jumps. It's for giving as well as taking (depending on whose need is uppermost at the time) and for sharing, laughing, problem-solving, soothing, salving, reassuring and getting along. It is also, still, just as they say in the old marriage books (do they still have those?), for mystical union, and don't let anyone tell you any different.

Back in Style
The women's magazines, the litmus paper of the attitudes and mores of our time, have stopped all that nonsense about the thrill of the one-night stand, the weekend cruise, the Riviera fling or the blue-collar bang. Even *Cosmopolitan* magazine is getting as serious as it is capable of getting about it. Here are two recent article titles with a hint of their contents:

- 12 Types of Sexual Husbands – "Recognize anyone you know?"
- When Your Sexual Styles Don't Mesh – "Lulls are normal in long-term liaisons."

The fact that these are aimed at "long-term liaisons" reveals a real change in attitude from the swinging sixties and self-fulfilling seventies. Something else has changed, too – the divorce rate. It has finally slowed and shows some indication of continuing to decrease. So. Divorce is out; babies are in. Sex in marriage (like marriage itself?) is here to stay. What married people have to do now is find time for it.

Organized Sex
Where and how do you fit sex into the schedule of a busy couple, and who has the energy anyway? The magazines have been busy with that one, too, being careful not to sound too much like Total Woman. Remember Marabel Morgan suggesting you meet your husband at the door wearing nothing but a frilly apron and a smile, put a candle on the floor and make love under the dining room table? The trouble with that scenario wasn't that it was so silly (which it was) or that the kids would laugh (which they would), but that it's treating each other as objects. The wife presents herself as object to be

consumed; she handles her husband like object to be manipulated. But these busy days, if you don't make it happen, if you don't organize it, weeks could go by without making love.

It's not only lack of time. The presence of children can be inhibiting. Kids get embarrassed when mothers and fathers are lovey-dovey (but not as upset as when they fight and yell and throw things.) You need privacy as well as time. So you have to get organized.

Afternoon Delight and Other Times

A teenager looked at me archly a few years back when the song "Afternoon Delight" was on the charts and asked me if I knew what that meant. Yes, I said, I believed I did. Each generation always thinks it invented sex. In my day, they were called nooners, and they were difficult but not impossible to arrange. Sadly, such delight is easily arranged by people indulging in extra-marital affairs. I am told that the afternoon business in big-city hotels would astonish me. Can you imagine a husband and wife booking into a hotel for an afternoon?

Yes, I can. And if there's no other time and no other private space, don't hesitate. You have to make the time. If you don't, the threat goes, someone else will. These days, the threat can be made to either spouse. Such a break from the usual routine can be a powerful aphrodisiac. It can also be very restful, afterwards, if you indulge in an afternoon nap.

Morners are fine, too, but depend more on the matching of the couple's body-times than on waiting till the kids leave the house. If one is a lark and the other is a nightingale, then it's harder to bring off because the nightingale is barely functioning before noon.

Some nights you'll have to do a little programming: easy dinner, early lights out (harder and harder as the kids get older and older), no projects, no work, just extra time for each other, giving your mate your absolutely undivided attention, and vice, I'm happy to say, versa.

Quick jumps have their place (not on the ironing board

again!) but do not supply the other valuable activity that making love paves the way for – conversation.

Pillow Talk

The kind of communication that goes on before and after (also during, if you like to talk about what's going on and how it feels) sex is one of the most valuable a marriage can offer and is one of the great cementers of the family. This is a free, open and trusting time, uninterrupted, private and loving. As I say, valuable. Use it well.

I can't resist ending with Mae West's line: "The best way to hold a man is in your arms."

CHAPTER TWENTY–FIVE

What is Marriage For?

If love is the answer, could you rephrase the question? — *Lily Tomlin*

In spite of all the freebies and the availability of outside sources for most of the services that used to be provided by the family, sociologists agree that there are two things that marriage and the family provide that cannot compare with scab efforts: parenthood and companionship.

Companionship

Companionship is a slow, long-flowering bloom that, set in the best soil, will continue to offer pleasure until evening (old age) or the twilight of the gods (death), whichever comes first. Hand-in-hand-into-the-sunset is a cliché based on gut-level truth. Happily married people will tell you that they are married to their best friend. Their friendship remains the most important thing in their lives and enables them to weather all upheavals, good or bad, because they face them together. Looking into another's eyes romantically may provide a short-term thrill, and we can all use it. Gazing outward together provides focus and assurance and long-term comfort. By that outward gaze, I really mean a metaphorical one – looking at one's goals – but it's valuable on a simpler level, too. One widow told me after her first big trip after her husband died that the magnificent view she looked at put her into a deep depression, "Because," she said, "I didn't have David looking at it with me." Sharing precious moments is one of the most important facets of any friendship. With a life-long companion such sharing has a cumulative effect. Haven't you noticed people who have been together a long time glance at each other and smile at some little happening? There are layers and layers of perception, understanding, pleasure and memory in a glance like that.

"It's easy to make new friends," an old friend said to me, a long time ago now, "but impossible to make old ones." Old friends take time. So do old companions, life-companions. They're worth hanging on to.

Some of My Best Friends

I may at times have sounded strident in this book, irritated at some of the inequities women suffer both in and out of marriage in what is still a patriarchal society. I want you to know I really like men. (Let it be understood right off the top that I am not talking about men who hurt women, or children, or other men, for that matter.) Some of my best friends are men. I was married to a kind, funny, magic man, and I still miss him. My father was a real patriarch of the old school, but he was also my very good friend. I have two sons, quite different from each other, and I love them both dearly, too. I have been disappointed and disillusioned by a number of men, but perhaps I expected too much of them because I had such high standards of comparison. (I have been disappointed by women, too.) I do not wish ill to any man. The best ones are already nurturers. I want them to go on growing and changing as they must, as women change. The best thing a man and woman can do for their family is to nurture each other. And be friends.

Marriage Is Something Else

Men like marriage better than women. On being asked whether they would marry again, the majority of women in a survey say they would not; men say they would – and prove it when they get the chance. American sociologist Jessie Bernard discovered that in every marriage there are two marriages: his and hers. His is happier than hers is. On happiness scales, married men are the happiest, single men the most unhappy; single women are happier than married women.

Fourteen Good Things About Marriage

This is not to say that marriage is a bad thing. Here are fourteen good things about marriage:

- Private jokes.
- Unlimited touching.
- Bathroom humour.
- Curfews – someone to make you live a regular life.
- Holidays, even short ones, like an hour off to go for a walk, drink coffee or wine, see a movie (husbands are very time-consuming!).
- Reading – not only someone to share things in the paper with but also to read maps, travelogues and recipes with.
- Warmth – especially feet in bed.
- Kissing.
- Talking – all night when you both get excited about an idea.
- Service above and beyond the call – someone to go the extra mile when you can't.
- Sharing (you name it).
- Mutual serfdom – someone to spoil and pamper and to be spoiled and pampered by.
- Cooking together.
- Loving.

Marriage As Art

I could write an entire essay on marriage without saying a word myself: just quote the great and not-so-great minds of this planet on what they thought marriage was and leave it for you to sort out. It's odd that out of the hundreds of good lines about marriage that I have come across I should choose the definition of an Ottawa lawyer, from an article in which he was discussing marriage contracts. What Douglas Adams has realized, in defining marriage as "essentially an art form," is the amorphous quality of marriage. It's an organism that defies being nailed down, pinned and wriggling, to be dissected, sliced and put under a microscope for observation. It is more complex than the sum of its myriad parts; it keeps growing and changing before your very eyes and heart.

How to Live Happily Ever After

Why discuss marriage, anyway, in a book about the family? Because marriage is to family what legs are to a table. Marriage is for family, though it can be for other things as well; family is not for marriage, though some people don't get married until they have a family. Marriage is the agreement to let a family happen.

Give me an argument. Families can exist without marriage, without children even. Clusters of people who band together for self-interest and self-protection do indeed comprise a kind of family, and married people without children are considered families. Families are simply a bunch (or a pair) of people who live together and try to get along. But – and this is why we still get stuck in the biological imperatives and all the stereotyped roles that have their roots in the primordial mud – there is one equation we take as written in stone:

Love + Marriage + Children = Family

Granted, the love connection is a fairly recent (maybe 150 years old) idea and complicates things. People of other centuries would ask, "What has love got to do with marriage?"

The Changing Reasons for Marriage

Initially, marriage was for property, to get it and to keep it in the family – yes, family. So marriage was for blood lines, keeping the genes in the family. Marriage started getting soft around the edges about the same time that childhood and motherhood were invented. By Victorian times sentiment was in full bloom, fed and fertilized by a compost heap of other behaviour. Love, of course, is not a twentieth-century idea; romantic love has its roots in chivalry, dating from about the thirteenth century. But love as a prerequisite of marriage and the Krazy Glue that holds it and the family together – *that's* twentieth-century. Today marriages are made in heaven and Hollywood, and love is what makes the marriage go round.

Love – the perceived necessity of, the maintenance of, the fading of and the transference of – has put tremendous pressure on the twentieth-century family. Margaret Mead, my favourite anthropologist, commented: "The [American] marriage is one of the most difficult marriage forms that the human race has ever attempted." And feminist writer Germaine Greer has added: "The nuclear family is possibly the shortest-lived familial system ever developed." Well, we knew that – poor old 4 to 7 percenters. But radiating out from that epicentre of the fifties and sixties that most of us raised children in or grew up in is an ideal of family that we haven't relinquished, and I guess love is the reason for it all, and marriage is the means.

Making Marriage Work

Here's what you need:

- Equality. Marriage is supposed to be an equal partnership. Just remember that some partners are more equal than others. A fine Ukrainian gentleman, a friend of my husband's, took us to lunch before we were married and gave us some advice. "Marriage," he said, "is not a fifty-fifty proposition. It's sixty-forty. If both of you give sixty, you'll be okay."
- Laughter. Laugh a lot. Keep laughing. A bunch of us newlyweds were going around the room asking each in turn why he or she married. "For laughs," my husband said, and we all laughed.
- Bed. I know one couple who have been married for forty years and both husband and wife attribute their longevity to a "cheap physical attraction." They still lust after each other.
- Pillow talk. Yeah, yeah, I know, he just rolls over and goes to sleep, but there are still lots of times you can catch him

awake and willing to chat. Some talk may be purely practical, like who's going to take the car in for an oil change and when will you have Mother for dinner and what will we say to Jason's teacher? But some of it is pure flying fantasy, hopes and dreams and speculations, recollections and reveries, all the intimate, shining threads and delicate stitches that create the seamless, weatherproof marriage robe.

- Upright conversation. That's not bad, either. If you've found someone you can get zapped by an idea with and sit up and talk to all night, hang on tight. A marriage is really a nonstop conversation. If the conversation stops, you're in trouble.

- Loyalty. Remember that line, "My country right or wrong"? Well, it's my mate, right or wrong. But . . .

- Truth. If he or she is wrong, be truthful and courageous and loyal enough to say so – in private. "Dear, you're drinking/eating/smoking/working too much. I'll help you stop." This is not easy and works only if the lines of communication are really open.

- Creativity. We've already acknowledged that marriage is an art form. It didn't get that way by being boxed in, wrapped up, tied tightly and put in a vault for preservation. This is a living, breathing, changing organism. So live, breathe and change with it. Together.

- Surprise. This is like creativity, but different. If you retain the ability to surprise your mate, it means you're still developing separately as human beings, that you haven't become a carbon copy of the other, that you keep finding new things in yourself, and therefore in your marriage.

- Fidelity. There are all kinds of ways of being unfaithful, not the worst of them with your body. Fidelity has to do with trust given and granted, with time and attention, and with follow-through, day by day by day by day.

Six Marriages

Mel Krantzler is a marriage counsellor who decided after he divorced and remarried that one marriage is enough for most people. "I learned," he says, "that divorce need not be the answer for couples of good will . . . who value what they have, or had, but want something more out of their present relationship." Krantzler has identified a sequence of six stages of marriage. He says that a couple who anticipate, identify and prepare themselves for each of these stages can cope with them successfully.

1. The Now We Are a Couple marriage. Honeymoon, dreams, plans, also shocks, revelations, anxiety. I think today's newlyweds are even more uptight than we were in my day because they see so many casualties all around them. They're desperate to be different, to make this marriage the one that lasts. This stage lasts about three years, according to Krantzler.

2. The What's Happening to My Career? marriage. Juggling a career and a spouse is not easy because there are conflicting schedules, not to say loyalties. Both marriage and career require enormous physical and emotional investments. Krantzler says people may begin to feel that "their obligations to their spouse are holding them back from greater job success and happiness." I say, define success and happiness.

3. The Here We Are Parents marriage. You think (insanely) that a child won't change your life (or you), but of course it does. The living organism changes shape and re-forms to incorporate another living organism. And baby makes three. Sometimes it feels like six.

4. The Suddenly We're Older marriage. If I had a nickel for every man who said he didn't mind being a grandfather but he hated the thought of sleeping with a grandmother, I'd start a fund for retired grandmothers. You have to come to terms with some of your dreams that aren't ever going to come true and with your compromises, and that includes the dream of the marriage you hoped for and the compromise with the good working model you developed.

5. The Is the Past My Only Future? marriage. Oddly enough, this has become more dangerous than in other generations. It's the time of the male menopause and the mid-life dump, L'Oréal, a face-lift (if one can afford it and is not philosophically opposed to it) and all the denial of

the aging process that people in a society devoted to youth go through.

6. The Summing Up marriage. "Was it all worthwhile?" My grandfather married my grandmother when she was seventeen and he was nineteen. She died before he did, in her late seventies (young for our family). The day of her funeral he looked at her in her coffin, so old and white, and said, "Doesn't she look like a young girl – so beautiful?" He turned his chair to the window and gazed out in the direction of the cemetery until he died.

It *is* worthwhile.

APPENDIX

1 Information

Join the Vanier Institute of the Family and receive their quarterly magazine, *Transition*, and keep up with the changing world of families. Individual memberships cost $15, but membership is available free of charge to those who find the fee a financial burden.

The Vanier Institute of the Family
120 Holland Avenue
Ottawa, Ontario K1Y 0X6

If you have a particular problem, or even a (morbid) curiosity, get a copy of the Advisory Council on the Status of Women's book on family law: *Family Law in Canada: New Directions*, November 1985. Write to them at:

Advisory Council on the Status of Women
Box 1541, Station B
Ottawa, Ontario K1P 5R5

The twenty-two-page brief, *A Fair Chance For All Children*, is available for $3 from:

The Child Poverty Action Group
950 Yonge St., Ste. 1000
Toronto, Ontario M4W 2J4

2 Sunday Breakfast
BUTTERMILK PANCAKES
Stir 1 teaspoon of salt and 2 teaspoons of baking soda into 2 cups of flour, add 2 cups of buttermilk and mix lightly. Break two eggs into the mixture, but don't stir yet, except to break the yolks. Melt together 2 tablespoons of honey and 2 tablespoons of butter and stir into the mixture, blending well but not too much – it doesn't matter if it's a little lumpy. If the batter seems thick (it usually is), stir in a couple tablespoons cold water. Drop by spoonfuls, or quarter-cups, onto a hot griddle. Turn once. (They say you should turn pancakes when you can count twelve bubbles on the top.) Serve with butter and syrup to the family you love.

3 Rate Your Marriage
Here's another list from an article entitled "Measure Your Marriage Potential, A Simple Test," prepared by David R. and Vera C. Mace for the January 1978 issue of *The Family Co-Ordinator* magazine. You rate on a scale of one to ten these areas in your marriage relationship:
1. Common goals and values
2. Commitment to growth
3. Communication skills
4. Creative use of conflict
5. Appreciation and affection
6. Agreement on gender roles
7. Co-operation and team work
8. Sexual fulfillment
9. Money management
10. Parent effectiveness

4 How to Keep Love Alive
There are no guarantees, but skillful application of the points in this list (from the Brandens' *Romantic Love Question and Answer Book*) might help your marriage.
• express love verbally
• express love sexually

- be physically affectionate
- create time to be alone together
- express appreciation and admiration
- participate in mutual self-disclosure
- offer your mate an emotional support system
- express love materially
- accept demands and put up with shortcomings

BIBLIOGRAPHY

Books
* = Recommended

Baker, Maureen. *The Family: Changing Trends in Canada*. Toronto: McGraw-Hill Ryerson, 1984.

Bel Geddes, Joan. *How to Parent Alone: A Guide for Single Parents*. New York: The Seabury Press, 1974.

Berne, Eric. *Games People Play*. New York: Grove Press, 1964.

* Blumstein, Philip, and Schwartz, Pepper. *American Couples, Money, Work, Sex*. New York: William Morrow, 1983.

Boulding, Elsie. *The Underside of History*. Boulder, CO: Westview Press, 1976.

Cavan, Ruth Shonle, ed. *Marriage and the Family in the Modern World*. New York: Crowell, 1974.

DeMause, Lloyd, ed. *The History of Childhood*. New York: The Psychohistory Press, 1974.

Dickson, Paul. *The Official Rules*. New York: Delacorte Press, 1978.

* Ephron, Nora. *Funny Sauce: Us, the Ex, the Ex's New Mate, The New Mate's Ex, and the Kids*. New York: Viking, 1986.

Forcey, Linda. *Mothers and Sons: Toward an Understanding of Responsibility*. Boston, Toronto: Little, Brown, & Co., 1983.

Gilbreth, Lillian; Thomas, Orpha Mae; Clymer, Eleanor. *Management in the Home*. New York: Dodd, Mead & Co., 1959.

Hample, Naomi. *Hugging, Hitting, and Other Family Matters*. New York: The Dial Press, 1979.

Howe, Louise Kapp, ed. *The Future of the Family*. New York: Simon & Schuster, 1972.

* Kaye, Kenneth. *Family rules: How to Help Your Children Grow Up Happy, Self-Respecting, and Responsible*. New York: Walker, 1984.

* Kome, Penney. *Somebody Has To Do It: Whose Work Is Housework?* Toronto: McClelland & Stewart, 1982.

Kornhaber, Arthur, and Woodward, Kenneth L. *Grandparents, Grandchildren: The Vital Connection*. Garden City, NY: Anchor Press/Doubleday, 1981.

Krantzler, Mel. *Creative Divorce*. New York: NAL, 1975.

———. *Creative Marriage*. New York: McGraw-Hill, 1981.

Laing, R.D. *The Politics of the Family*. Massey Lectures, 1968. Toronto: CBC Learning Systems, 1974.

Larson, Lyle E., ed. *The Canadian Family in Comparative Perspective*. Scarborough, ON: Prentice-Hall, 1976.

Lapham, Lewis; Pollan, Michael, and Etheridge, Eric. *The Harper's Index Book*. New York: Henry Holt, 1987.

Lasch, Christopher. *Haven in a Heartless World*. New York: Basic Books, 1983.

———. *The Minimal Self: Psychic Survival in Troubled Times*. New York: W.W. Norton, 1984.

Laser, Michael, and Goldner, Ken. *Children's Rules for Parents*. Don Mills, ON: Stoddart; New York: Harper & Row, 1987.

Maddox, Brenda. *The Half-Parent: Living with Other People's Children*. New York: M. Evans, 1975.

* Maslin, Bonnie, and Nir, Yehuda. *Not Quite Paradise, Making Marriage Work*. New York: Doubleday, 1987.

McQuade, Walter, and Aikman, Ann. *Stress: What It Is/What It Can Do To Your Health/How to Fight Back*. New York, Toronto: Bantam Books, 1975.

Mead, Margaret. *Culture and Commitment*. 1970. Updated. New York: Columbia University Press, 1978.

———. *Male and Female: A Study of the Sexes in a Changing World*. 1949. Reprint. New York: William Morrow, 1967.

Mead, Margaret, and Heyman, Ken. *Family*. New York: MacMillan, 1965.

Mead, Margaret, and Métraux, Rhoda. *Aspects of the Present*. New York: William Morrow, 1980.

Millar, Thomas P. *The Omnipotent Child*. Palmer Press, Cloverdale, BC: D.W. Friesen & Sons, 1983.

Minden, Dr. Harold A. *Two Hugs for Survival: Strategies for Effective Parenting*. Toronto: McClelland & Stewart, 1982.

Otto, Herbert, A., ed. *The Family in Search of a Future*. New York: Appleton-Century-Crofts, 1970.

Packard, Vance. *Our Endangered Children: Growing Up in a Changing World*. Boston, Toronto: Little, Brown, 1983.

* Peck, Ellen, and Granzig, W. *The Parent Test: How to Measure and Develop Your Talent for Parenthood*. New York: G.P. Putnam's Sons, 1977.

* Pogrebin, Letty Cottin. *Family Politics: Love and Power on an Intimate Frontier*. Toronto, New York: McGraw-Hill, 1983.

* Postman, Neil. *The Disappearance of Childhood*. New York: Dell, 1982.

Rhodes, Sonya, and Wilson, Josleen. *Surviving Family Life: The Seven Crises of Living Together*. New York: G.P. Putnam's Sons, 1981.

Rice, Robin D. *The American Nanny*. New York: Harper & Row, 1987.

Russell, Bertrand. *Marriage and Morals*. London: Unwin, 1972.

Selye, Hans. *The Stress of Life*. Toronto, New York: McGraw-Hill, 1976.

Siegel-Gorelick, Bryna. *The Working Parents' Guide to Child Care: How to Find the Best Care for Your Child*. Boston: Little, Brown, 1983.

Shorter, Edward. *The Making of the Modern Family*. New York: Basic Books, 1975.

Slung, Michele. *More Momilies*. New York: Ballantine, 1986.

Stein, Richard A. *Personal Strategies for Living With Stress*. New York: John Gallagher Communications, 1983.

Stinnett, Nick, and Birdsong, Craig Wayne. *The Family and Alternate Life Styles*. Chicago: Nelson-Hall, 1978.

Stock, Gregory. *The Book of Questions*. New York: Workman Publishing, 1987.

* Strommen, Merton P., and Strommen, A. Irene. *Five Cries of Parents*. Toronto: Fitzhenry and Whiteside; San Francisco: Harper & Row, 1985.

Sweet, O. Robin, and Siegel, Mary-Ellen. *The Nanny Connection: How to Find and Keep a Perfect Nanny*. New York: Atheneum, 1987.

Toffler, Alvin. *Future Shock*. New York: Bantam Books, 1980.

Wahlroos, Sven. *Family Communication: A Guide to Emotional Health*. New York: Macmillan, 1974.

* Walker, Glynnis. *Second Wife, Second Best?* Toronto: Doubleday Canada, 1984.

Wylie, Betty Jane, and MacFarlane, Lynne. *Everywoman's Money Book*. Toronto: Key Porter Books, 1985.

Brochures and Pamphlets

Advisory Council on the Status of Women:
  Battered But Not Beaten, 1987
Family Law in Canada: New Directions, 1985
Integration & Participation: Women's Work in the Home and in the Labour Force
Love, Marriage and Money, 1984
Wife Battering in Canada: the Vicious Circle, 1980
Boulding, Elsie, "Learning and the Familial Society: The Place of the Family in Times of Transition." Ottawa: The Vanier Institute of the Family, 1981.
Economic Council of Canada:
  The Changing Economic Status of Women, 1984
Marriage, Population, and the Labour Force Participation of Women, 1984
  Statistics Canada:
  Canada's Families, 1979
Canada's Lone-Parent Families, 1984
Canada's Young Family Home-Owners, 1984
Current Demographic Analysis: Report on the Demographic Situation in Canada, 1986
Divorce: Law and the Family in Canada, 1983
Families (by Structure and Type)
Family History Survey, 1985
Lone Parenthood: Characteristics and Determinants, 1986
Women in the Workplace
Women in the Work World

Articles

Arond, Miriam, and Pauker, Samuel L. "How Marriage Changes Your Sex Life (but does it have to?)" *New Woman* (October 1987). Excerpted from *The First Year of Marriage* (New York: Warner Books, 1987).

212 ALL IN THE FAMILY

Bernard, Jessie. "Special Report: The Future of Women and Marriage." *The Futurist* (April 1970).

Berton, Paul (plus files of others). "Wanted: Mary Poppins." *Maclean's* (November 10, 1986).

Blakely, Mary Kay. "Postnuclear Family." *Ms* (July/August 1987).

Branson, Anne-Marie. "Confessions of a Not-so-Wicked Stepmother." *New Woman* (June 1987).

Cornish, Edward. "The Future of the Family: Intimacy in an Age of Loneliness." *The Futurist*, Vol. 13, no. 1 (February 1979).

Kantrowitz, Barbara, et al. "A Mother's Choice." *Newsweek* (March 31, 1986).

Keller, Suzanne. "Does the Family Have a Future?" *Journal of Comparative Studies*, Vols. 1-2 (Spring 1977).

Lennon, Rosemarie. "The Plight of the Second Wife." *New Woman* (September 1987).

Levoy, Gregg. "Is Anyone Listening?" *Toronto Star* (December 10, 1987).

McHugh, Mary. "Ten Major Reasons Why Women Get Divorced." *Cosmopolitan* (May 1987).

Ms. "The Blended Family." Special edition (February 1985).

Newsweek. "How to Stay Married." Special (August 24, 1987).

Pines, Maya. "Restoring Law and Order in the Family." Interview with family therapist Jay Haley, *Psychology Today* (November 1982).

Ramey, James W. "Intimate Networks: Will They Replace the Monogamous Family?" *The Futurist*, Vol. 9 (August 1975).

Webb, Marilyn. "Back to the Nest: Grown Up Children Who Move Back In." *New York* magazine (February 1, 1988).

1272   2390